Don't Draw Back:

ALLOW LIFE'S STORMS TO MAKE YOU BETTER!

RICK CREEL

Don't Draw Back: Allow Life's Storms to Make You Better!

Cover image by Pam Creel.

DEDICATION

I dedicate this book to my wonderful Savior and Healer, Jesus Christ. I am forever grateful for His Word that has truly been "a lamp unto my feet, and a light unto my path." Psalm 119:105

Also, to my amazing wife, Pam. She is such a rock when it comes to spiritual battles but such a beautiful and compassionate person in every way. I love her with all my heart!

CONTENTS

INTRODUCTION

My favorite scripture is Hebrews 10:38, "Now the just shall live by faith; But if anyone draws back, my soul has no pleasure in him." However, my favorite part of that scripture is probably not what you would think. It's the part "b" of the verse about drawing back. The words "draw back" are a nautical term that means "take in your sail." I've come to learn many times in life when we are tempted to "take in our sails"—these are the very times we need to hoist them high to catch the wind of God's Spirit to propel us forward in ways that we never dreamed or imagined!

1 BUILDING THE SHEPHERD'S HOUSE

In May of 2019, I noticed I had an unusual cough. It wasn't like a normal "clear your throat" kind of cough. It was persistent, lasting longer than normal. *"Hum,"* I thought, *"That was kind of strange."* I was on a building site in northern Alabama where Pam, my wife, and I were building our dream lake house. After a few years of dreaming, calculating costs, and making plans, we had finally taken the plunge to make our dream a reality. We decided to call it "The Shepherd's House." Taken from Psalm 23, our goal was to provide a place where family, friends, and even people we didn't know could come, relax and just have fun!

We were in the final stages of completion and finally moved in the first of August. We were so excited! Our long-awaited vision and dream had happened! It had been something the Lord had placed in my heart a few years back and I had journaled these thoughts in 2016:

I see in my mind and feel in my spirit a beautiful lake home-a beautiful dock—pristine, everything in its place, everything in order. But it's not just a lake home...it's a refuge, it's a war room. It's a place of deliverance; it's a place where marriages are restored. A place where troubled marriages, troubled people, troubled couples can be refreshed, renewed and restored!! A place where there's fun, fellowship, music, songs, worship, teaching, small groups, and most importantly, the Holy Spirit lifting burdens and breaking the yoke of bondage.

Little by little the coughing continued. While I really didn't know what was going on with me, I dismissed it as something that I hoped would soon pass. By the fall of that year, Pam began to question me about the coughing. "I don't know," I would say. I started trying cough drops. They seemed to help minimize the urge to cough. It was especially nagging right after I would eat. Finally, in December, I visited a gastroenterologist. I explained everything that was going on as well as I could. I told him that I had this persistent cough. In addition, I told him that I seemed to run out of air as I would talk, and this also triggered coughing. The doctor ordered a chest X-ray and then an endoscopy for early January 2020. The X-ray came back normal showing nothing out of the ordinary.

After the holidays, I went in for the endoscopy procedure. Upon completion, the doctor informed Pam that everything looked fine other than some redness in my throat. He assured her that while he knew we were concerned, he thought everything was okay. He prescribed some acid reflux medicine and wanted me to return in three months. After taking the medicine daily as prescribed, I didn't notice any improvement at all. In fact, as time went on, things got worse.

By now, it was April of 2020. Of course, everyone knows what happened in the spring of 2020! Covid 19 was sweeping through the world creating a pandemic like most of us had never seen. I was coughing more and more and had even started wheezing with deep breaths. I tried to make an appointment with a pulmonary doctor that had performed a sleep study and diagnosed me with sleep apnea some six years earlier. He was no longer at that facility and the pandemic had created extra precautions that made it difficult to see even any doctor! Luckily, our company had suspended most of us from traveling. I am a manufacturing engineer that works from home. Most all of my work involves traveling to our various facilities on a regular basis.

By the time May rolled around, it was warming up outside. One Saturday while at the Shepherd's house, (our lake home), my wife, daughter, future son-in-law, and I, took a ride on our pontoon boat over to the marina for lunch. We docked there and ate on the boat that beautiful spring day. While eating, I noticed that I could barely swallow the hamburger I had ordered. At first, I just dismissed it as nothing...maybe too big of a bite. However, as I continued eating, I knew it was something else. Every bite felt like it would barely go down. I didn't say anything to anyone about it until later.

May was also the time for my annual physical. Upon visiting my primary care physician, I told him everything that was going on. He is a very kind man and told me to visit an ENT, (ear, nose & throat doctor), and if I didn't get the results that I needed, to visit a pulmonary doctor. I took his advice and soon made an appointment with an ENT. During that visit, the doctor listened to my concerns and ran a scope up my nose and down my throat. He said he didn't see anything wrong but ordered a CT scan of my neck and head. He also prescribed a variety of medicines thinking it could be late-onset asthma or allergies. He prescribed an inhaler, something I had never taken before. The inhaler did seem to help some.

As May turned into June, my job demands were starting to increase. I had scheduled a trip to one of our facilities early that month. When I returned, my son and daughter-in-law picked me up at the airport. During the short ride home, I coughed and coughed. Later, my son referred back to that night saying that I coughed all the way home. My family knew something was not right with me!

Over the next week or so, I was doing everything prescribed. By now, as the cough continued, there was some (I know this is gross) mucus building up as I coughed. Obviously, I was very concerned about my health; I paid attention to what I was coughing up. One morning while out on the deck during my devotion time, the coughing started. My routine has always been to get some coffee first, then go out on our deck and have my devotion time. As usual, as soon as I started to drink the coffee the coughing would start...relentless was this cough! That morning, however, was different. That morning while coughing, I noticed a tiny speck of blood! I took a picture with my phone, then went in the house and told Pam, "Something is wrong with me!" I told her that it was scaring me! She told me to not be frightened, but that we needed to keep looking for a doctor that could help. Immediately, I began searching for the best pulmonary doctor in our city. I called to make an appointment and the wait was two months! I told the receptionist that I could not wait that long. She said, "Well, there's another doctor that can see you in a few days." I asked her to please put me down for the appointment!

Prior to getting in to actually talk to the doctor, she had ordered an X-ray and a full-blown breathing test. For this test, I sat in a small booth and blew into a tube connected to a computer. I followed the instructions of the technician to check out my lung capacity. After round one, she had me use an inhaler and then retake the test. "You performed significantly better after the inhaler," she said at the conclusion of the test. Afterwards, I visited the pulmonary doctor. I told her everything that was going on with me up to this point: the relentless coughing, the wheezing, the trouble swallowing, and the latest issue, coughing up blood. Her response was, "You know you have asthma, don't you?" I said, "No one had ever told me that before." She said, "Well, you do." I then told the doctor that in researching asthma, I had discovered that while you do cough, you don't cough up blood. She went on to tell me, "That's true, but if you have coughed as much as you have described, your throat is probably irritated." She then took her light and inspected my throat. "Yep, it's red. I didn't see anything in the chest x-ray. I'm going to change your inhaler, and give you a drug specifically for asthma. However, because you told me about the blood, I'm going to schedule a CT scan just to check things out."

The next week (now late June 2020), the CT scan was set. I went alone. I remember being a bit anxious while waiting that day. As my name was called, I entered a room where there was a narrow padded table just in front of a round looking device. I was instructed to lie down. "Have you ever had a contrast before?" "No ma'am," I answered. She then went on to explain the sensation I would feel as it entered my body intravenously. "You will feel very warm; then the sensation will travel down your body and you may feel like you have to urinate." I remember thinking that I wished Pam had come with me. I didn't realize they were going to give me something like this...it was unnerving. "Raise your arms and keep them behind your head until we're done." The circular scanner then started up, swirling around me like a tunnel. I was instructed to hold my breath as I entered the tunnel until each scan was complete. After removing the IV, the technician said, "We're all done. Someone will contact in the next few days to let you know the results." As I got up, I tried hard to read her body language. I remember thinking, *I wonder if she saw something and just doesn't want to tell me.*

A couple of days passed and now it was Thursday, July 2nd. We had planned a big July 4th weekend, and several family members were coming up to the lake to visit. Pam had gone on ahead of me that day as some family were getting there early. I came up a little later that afternoon. On the way up, I stopped to get some gas in the car. I happened to notice that I had a missed call. A voice message was left: "Mr. Creel, this is Dr. B, I have the results from the scan a few days ago. If you could call me back, that would be great." *Wow*, I thought, *how did I miss that call?* Wondering what the results were, I kept driving to the Shepherd's house. Then my phone rang. "Mr. Creel, this is Dr. B, can you talk a few minutes?" "Yes, Ma'am," I said nervously. As she began talking to me, I pulled into a parking lot on the way. "We found a knot in your left lung and some swollen lymph nodes in your chest." I could hardly believe what she was saying to me! How could this be happening? "I hate to give you this news right before

5

a holiday, but they will be contacting you today because we need to perform a bronchoscopy. My assistant will call you to set it up, and I didn't want you to be unaware as to why she is contacting you. We will have a pathologist in the operating room to take samples to determine what it is." I tried to be strong as she asked, "Do you have anything you want to ask me?" "How big is the knot?" I asked. "Well, I don't really have anything to reference the size, but it's 3.5 centimeters," she responded. "I don't suppose you want to speculate as to what it might be until you've had a chance to evaluate things," I asked her. "No, I need to take a look at things first," she replied. I thanked her for calling. As I sat in my car that afternoon, stunned at what had just transpired, I remember saying to the Lord, "You are my life...I trust You."

Upon arriving at the Shepherd's House, there were many people in and out as family had started to gather for the upcoming holiday. I took my bags in the house, greeted a couple of folks, and quietly motioned for Pam to come out into the garage. I told Pam that the doctor had called and filled her in on the conversation with the doctor. I told Pam what I had said to the Lord, that I trusted Him. I also told her that our children would be watching how we respond to this. We also agreed that we would not tell anyone until the weekend had ended so we could talk to our immediate family first. You just have to know Pam. She is a very level-headed, Spirit-filled, wisdom-filled, praying rock that I am so fortunate to be married to! She reassured me that the Lord would be with us.

As the afternoon continued, there were nieces, nephews, parents, and children all wanting to take a boat ride. I somehow compartmentalized the bad news and acted as if nothing was wrong. As we loaded up the pontoon boat to go for a ride, the Lord gave me supernatural strength. I entertained the group and He kept my mind from trying to go to a bad place. Of course it never left me, and the news was constantly just under the surface of my fake smile and disposition. I am not a fake person at all, but I realized that this was not the time or place to unload all of the news we had just received.

Later that afternoon, as things began to quiet down a bit; I went out on the deck. Desperately, I thought to myself, "I just need something to hold to, I need something to help me!" I sat down, opened my phone to our church app, and began to read that day's One-Year-Bible devotion. I regularly read my Bible but at that time, I rarely read the One-Year-Bible app. That day, the devotion was about Hezekiah being faced with death. Here is the exact devotion from Pastor Larry Stockstill:

> *"In the midst of the terrible ordeals of life, we often don't know to whom we can turn. In 2 Kings, chapter 20, Hezekiah was facing death because a terrible sickness had attacked his body. To whom did he turn in his hour of need? The Word of God tells us that "he turned his face to the wall and prayed to the Lord" (v. 2).*
>
> *The "wall" represents the tower of the Lord. In his moment of desperate need, Hezekiah's eyes were no longer fixed on human methods and reports. The things of the world no longer distracted his vision. Rather, he raced to safety inside the tower of the Lord.*
>
> *The Lord heard his cry and instructed Isaiah to have Hezekiah's servants apply an ointment made from figs. They obeyed his command, and Hezekiah was healed. Because he had run to God, God heard his prayer, saw his tears, and added fifteen years to his life (vv. 5-6).*
>
> *The tower of the Lord is a supernatural tower. It is so strong that it can turn the sun backward ten degrees, a feat that boggles the mind when the laws of physics are considered. Leave your present fears behind and run into the tower of the Lord. It is the one place you are safe!"*

Obviously, I KNEW the Lord was speaking to me! I got up from where I was while reading this devotion and walked around the corner of the house so that no one would see me. It was so powerful, but it was just the beginning of the miraculous things that happened along the journey!

2 PREPARING TO FIGHT

As the Fourth of July weekend continued, my son and daughter-in-law had several of their friends up to the Shepherd's House; my daughter and her fiancé came as well. The Shepherd's House was bustling with people and activities. On Saturday, I was waiting to fix my plate as the troops lined up for lunch. My son came over and quietly asked me if I had heard the results of the CT scan. I tried to play things down and give him an answer, but I'm sure he saw right through my "hem-hawing" around. He can be relentless with his questions at times. Obviously, he wanted to know the truth about his dad! While it was not my plan to tell him about the latest just yet, his relenting got the best of me. "Yes, I heard back but we can talk about it later," I said. Of course he wanted to know more—and would not take no for an answer. Quietly, I said, "They found a knot on my left lung and some swollen lymph nodes in my chest." It was certainly not what he wanted to hear, especially on a weekend with his friends. I watched him that afternoon as he went upstairs to his room and disappeared for a while.

One of the hardest things I encountered through this whole experience was watching how my family responded to hearing various news and reports. I love them so much and I hated to be the one bringing such anguish and sadness to their lives. As their dad, I could see and sense their quietness, their questions; you can read between the lines and just know they are disturbed.

Later that night after most had gone to their rooms for the evening, my son came into our bedroom. He told us that what we had described was very serious. I knew he had been looking things up online and was letting us know what he had discovered. He knew that I had been experiencing problems swallowing and finally came out and said, "That's all part of it, Dad!" I said, "I know, Son, but I want you to know that I'm not going online to read all about this stuff. I'm not afraid. We're going to trust the Lord," trying my best to reassure him. He then put his arm around me and started to cry. I'm sure he was thinking about the consequences and so many unknowns.

The next day, Sunday, after breakfast, we watched church online. I continued to sense the Lord encouraging me through songs. Quietly, He was letting me know that He was aware, and I was confident that He was moving, working things out for us. As the weekend ended and all had left except immediate family, we all huddled at the front door in a group hug. Now, finally able to talk openly, my son told us that in the previous days he had been asking the Lord to challenge his faith. He knew this was the challenge of his life. He then prayed for me. What a special time when you have spent countless hours pouring into your children about the faithfulness of God to see them rise up and declare who HE IS over your life! I told them that when we built the Shepherd's House I never dreamed that I was building it for me! We all cried together and they told me they loved me and I told them the same.

Afterwards, we made our way back to our primary residence just over an hour away. I think Pam and I both were learning to rely on the Lord's peace, His power, and His presence like never before. The nurse had called earlier to let me know that the bronchoscopy had been set up and scheduled for Tuesday morning at 6am.

The next day I stayed busy much of the day. I don't remember having any fear or anxiety. Later that evening, Pam went to pick up pizza that we enjoyed while sitting in the sun on the back deck. Our close friends came by to pray for us as they had learned of the next day's procedure. It's just amazing how something like what was happening will bring family closer than ever.

That night, instead of watching the news or other programs that Pam and I ordinarily watched, we chose to watch worship videos on YouTube. This was something we would learn to do regularly in the coming months. That night as we sat together in our den watching a worship video produced by our church, we worshipped God as His presence filled our house! I will never forget the song, "You Are My God" by Highlands Worship. Here are just a few of the lyrics:

With all that I am will praise you

Maker of heaven and earth

I lift my hands in surrender

Jesus my God

As long as I live I will worship

Your love is better than life

Your favor will last for a lifetime

Jesus my God

Chorus: You are my God

O the wonder of your great love

Lord your presence is more than enough

I will fall at the foot of the cross

You are my God, You are my God.

Written by CJ Blount, John Larson and Tyler Wester

© 2018 Highlands Creative Publishing

Somewhere around that point in the song, the Holy Spirit overwhelmed me with His precious presence and deep in my innermost being, I heard the Spirit of God began to pray through me! Romans 8:26-27 says it like this: "Likewise the Spirit also helps in our weaknesses. For we do not know what we should pray for as we ought, but the Spirit Himself makes intercession for us with groanings which cannot be uttered. Now He who searches the hearts knows what the mind of the Spirit is, because He makes intercession for the saints according to the will of God." I turned to Pam and said these words: "I'm not afraid, Pam."

The next morning, Tuesday, July 7, 2020, we were up early and on our way to the hospital for the bronchoscopy procedure. The goal of the procedure was to determine what the knot in my left lung consisted of and why the lymph nodes were swollen in my chest. The pathologist would immediately examine the biopsies to determine what it was.

They finally took me back, gave me that wonderful gown you change into, and placed me in a holding room. Luckily, Pam got to be with me. After a while, I was given the notorious "don't care shot" to help me relax before they took me in for the procedure. Soon they were rolling me down the hall into the operating room where I saw some monitors and my pulmonary doctor greeting me with "Good morning, Mr. Creel." They placed a mask on me and instructed me to take several deep breaths. The next thing I knew I was waking up. The procedure was all done.

Back in the same room as before surgery, Pam was awaiting my return. Upon waking up, I noticed they had placed a stainless bowl on my chest. The first thing I did was start to cough up lots of blood from the biopsies taken. I remember still being under heavy sedation, like a heavy lead blanket was covering me, but I was conscious and could hear people talking. "It's just not fair, life's just not fair," I remember the nurse saying. "You will need to take him as soon as possible, the sooner the better, to oncology. We are getting it set up now and you should hear from them soon. If you haven't heard from them in the next few days you call them." Even though I was highly sedated, I knew what that meant. Somehow, it didn't devastate me like you might think. I think that it was part of the plan to start discussing things before I was completely awake. That seemed to somehow lighten the news of the diagnosis. I heard Pam telling the nurse "okay" as she was giving her the instructions for our next steps. I asked for some soda to drink in between spitting out the blood as I coughed. We didn't talk about anything, nor did I ask any questions. Again, I was pretty out of it, but still knew what was going on.

Later Pam told me that after the procedure, the doctor met with her to tell her what was found. "Adenocarcinoma, lung cancer," the doctor said. "I'm sorry." The doctor then showed Pam a picture of my two large bronchial tubes. One tube was completely open, the other completely closed. Pam then asked, "Can they operate on him? The doctor explained that it was inoperable. Pam couldn't believe what she was hearing and then asked where the bathroom was, as she needed to get somewhere away from everyone. She later told me that she went straight to the restroom and locked the door behind her. Backed up against the wall, she began to cry quietly at first, then the cries got louder as she slid down the wall to the floor wailing so loud that it echoed. She later told me, "If only Stone or Carman could have been with me while the doctor told what she had found...but there was no one...completely alone." Crying out to the Lord was her only hope for comfort to process this unexpected news. She soon found His sweet Spirit ministering to her and was finally able to stand up, wipe away the tears, and walk back to where I was waiting in recovery, trying to act as though everything was okay.

After about an hour, Pam was instructed to go get the car and pull around to the door. The nurse loaded me in a wheel chair and transported me to meet her. I will never forget that just before Pam was pulling up, the nurse patted me on the shoulder and asked, "Did you get all that we were talking about?" "Yes, ma'am," I replied. She then patted me again.

On the way home from the hospital, things were quiet. I was still feeling the effects of the anesthesia heavily. I asked Pam if she would stop at a fast food place to get me a strawberry milkshake because my throat was sore. As we were in the drive thru, I asked, "Pam, are you ok?" That was all it took to break the dam of emotion. She began to sob uncontrollably. By the time we got around to pay for the shake, Pam was still very distraught and searching for some change. I remember the girl behind the glass window seeing her condition and just waiving her on through..."it's okay," she said. I then told Pam that I knew what was going on and that I was okay. I really can't remember what else I said, but I remember what she said in response to me...something that I have never heard her say to me before, "You're the bravest man I know."

When we got home, our family was all there. When I walked in, I remember all my family members just watching me not really knowing what to say to me. I distinctly remember my future son-in-law having such red eyes from crying as he watched the sadness all around. Needless to say, it was a hard day at the Creel house—probably one of the most difficult of all time. I told everyone that I needed to go lie down. I went into the bedroom to try to sleep off the remaining anesthesia.

After lying in bed for maybe 30 or 40 minutes, I could not sleep. "How am I supposed to respond to this?" I thought. When something like cancer has been spoken to you, and you know from the symptoms that you have experienced for the last several months that things are getting worse, it is hard to process. But in spite of all that was happening, I got up and went into the kitchen. I sat down at the head of the table where I always sit. I reached for my Hebrew-Greek study Bible that I love so much. I then asked my son, Stone, and Dillon, (our future son-in-law), to join me at the table. I began to tell them what had happened at the Shepherd's House the day I found out about the knot in my lung. In addition, I told them what I read in the One Year Bible that day about Hezekiah being faced with death. I told them that I knew the Lord had spoken to me through that story and we were going to trust Him through it all. I told them that I was not afraid. I also told them that while I was lying in the bed, the Lord had reminded me that I had been a student of His word for many years (I taught Sunday school for many years and studied the Bible hours and hours). I went on to say that I felt like the Lord was telling me that I had been prepared for this attack of the enemy. I remember telling them that I had taught countless Sunday School lessons about the faithfulness of God, His healing power, His deliverance. Now that something like this had come against me, I shouldn't be surprised. I was sure the devil was saying, "Let's just see if you really believe all that stuff you've been teaching all these years!" I also told them that Satan and this disease would be defeated in the same way that I had been trained all these years, through God's Word!

I could tell that once they knew my disposition they felt better also. I believe it instilled faith in them that day as they saw my reaction. But let me stop right here and say I didn't do any of that through my strength or wisdom. The Lord had truly prepared me and I was just speaking the Truth like a good soldier. The Lord used me to set the tone and the atmosphere that day. We were not going to complain, whine and wallow in pity or say "why me?" No, we were going to fight! Better yet, the Lord was fighting for us and we would just learn to hold to His Almighty hand!

After setting the tone for how we would proceed given the news that we received that day, I later found this note that my son Stone had left me.

7/7/20

Dad-

I want you to know that I'm here for you. No matter the circumstances, I'm praying for your complete healing. I'm asking the Lord to stop any further growth of your sickness and that it has to cease and bow at the name of Jesus. That God's healing hand would be upon you and he would breathe healing inside your body. Every cancer cell must die and retreat at the powerful name of Jesus. God is for you, He has you in the palm of his hand and He will minister to your mind and spirit every day. I don't just speak healing, I declare it. I'm fighting with you on the front lines, I'm not afraid, are you? If Christ is for us who can be against us. God is about to move in our lives like we've never seen before. I'm certain that God is working and we have angels fighting for you in the heavenlies. There is no one like you and I can't wait for you to one day tell my kids the miracle that unfolded before our very eyes. I love you Dad! More than you will ever know. You are a true example of Christ. I'm so thankful for a dad like You!

-Stone

3 A GOOD SOLDIER

The next day we decided to go back up to the Shepherd's House. Upon arriving there, I knew that I needed to call and talk to my boss and tell him the latest. It was a difficult call and I found myself struggling each time that I explained what they had found. My boss, a very kind and understanding man, was quite taken back, (as were all of us), with the news of the diagnosis. "How long will you be out, Rick?" he asked. "I don't know," I replied. I was wondering if he might have been indirectly inquiring if I was going to be able to return at all. I asked my boss to tell my good friend and colleague about the diagnosis for me. I told him that it takes a lot out of me to tell this story repeatedly. I made sure that anytime I told anyone about what was going on with me, I always spoke from a place of faith and hope, not defeat. My boss marveled at how I was approaching this situation, the attitude we had and our faith.

Later, while walking around the lake property many thoughts went through my mind. As we described earlier, Pam and I had worked extra hard to keep things very neat and orderly. Much thought and work had gone into how the house and property was kept. My pastor often speaks about excellence, and how maintaining that kind of atmosphere puts people at ease. Now, as I walked around the property, I had thoughts like "How could this be happening? Surely this wasn't all for nothing." I learned long ago as a young Christian to be very careful about what I let my mind dwell on. However, such thoughts would cross my mind even though I soon dismissed them.

Later that afternoon, as Pam and I continued trying to make sense of it all, we called some of our very closest friends, the Andersons. David and Angela Anderson are not ordinary people. They are the real deal! Both are committed Christians we have known and loved for over twenty years. The scripture in Proverbs 27:17, "As iron sharpens iron so one man sharpens the countenance of another," describes our relationship well! We have spent countless hours talking about God and His faithfulness. Both of our families have seen the Lord move countless times in our lives. However, this time there was a new level of desperation as we sought their precious wisdom and counsel.

As we called them that afternoon and explained the situation, I will never forget what David said to me. "Rick, when a soldier goes into battle he doesn't look to the right or left. He does what he has been trained to do, fight! You can't stand for yesterday; you can't stand for tomorrow; God is in control of that. You can only stand today and control what thoughts you think and the words that come out of your mouth. Satan has to bow at every word from God." I was writing down everything David was telling me because I value his friendship so much. Everyone needs friends like the Andersons...meaningful, strong bonds that come alongside you in life and help you get through the tough times!

The next morning I decided to send an email to a large group of Christian friends that we knew would pray for us. I got the idea from reading a devotion in the one-year Bible from the day before. Here's the exact email:

Hello V-Team! By the way, that stands for Victory Team!

We have included you in this email because you are our friends and we are confident that you will hold us up in prayer as we fight this battle.

Pastor Larry Stockstill said it so accurately in his devotion yesterday,

In spiritual warfare, you must remember two things. First, you need to pray constantly while the battle is raging. Assemble a group who will commit to pray continually until the battle turns and the victory is won. Second, remember that the Lord is fighting against the enemy (1 Chronicles 5:22). Recognize that it is really not your battle, but the Lord's.

God and Satan are irreconcilable enemies, and God is as interested in your victory as you are. When you realize that God is actually fighting your battle, you will say to the enemy as David did to Goliath, "The Lord does not need weapons to rescue his people. It is his battle, not ours. The Lord will give you to us!" (1 Samuel 17:47).

Pam & I are scheduled to meet with the oncologist Friday to discuss treatment. We need God's wisdom to be upon Dr. W. as he reviews my case.

It is our intent to send out regular updates. Please just reply to "our email" and not "all" if you have a response as we do not want to overload everyone's email.

We love each of you and value your friendship & prayers. Thank you from the bottom of our hearts.

Rick & Pam

The next day we had our first visit with the oncologist. Pam and I waited anxiously in the room for the doctor to come in and meet with us. After a few minutes and a knock at the door, we were introduced to Dr. W. Pam and I both noticed how he seemed to shuffle his feet and appear apprehensive as he began delivering his prognosis of my condition. Finally, he started by asking, "What do you know about your condition?" We told him that we knew it was lung cancer, a tumor in my left lower lung and swollen lymph nodes in my chest. Dr. W. responded by saying, "Yes, and we believe the current state is stage three." Dr. W. said it was adenocarcinoma. He went on to say that lung cancer has changed in the last five years. Now, adenocarcinoma is found in about 80 percent of non-smokers. Very surprised by this statement, Pam asked, "What causes it?" "We don't know," responded Dr. W. He then asked me if I had ever smoked, to which I answered no. He then proceeded to tell us about the next steps, which would include a scan to determine the extent of the spread. We questioned him about the various types of scans and settled on a PET scan that would show any and all cancer activity in my body. Dr. W. also said that we needed to do an MRI to see if the cancer had spread to my brain in addition to vital organs, such as my liver or kidneys. Needless to say, it was a lot to take in and process. He had me sit up on the examination table so that he could listen to my lungs as I took deep breaths. I remembering him saying, "You seem pretty healthy." "I feel like I am," I responded. "I walk, I try to eat right, I'm trying to be very careful about my sugar intake given the situation." He didn't seem too concerned about what I ate. He did tell me that he was more concerned about my weight and bulking up as the coming days would be quite difficult. "We're going to throw a lot at this, so we need you to be as healthy as you can be."

The PET scan was scheduled for the next Friday. Pam and I were soon on our way back home. There wasn't much hope offered that day, nor was there much excitement in talking about the treatment. I just remember the weight and gravity of the situation. I had been careful not to ask too many questions regarding life expectancy or chemo expectations. I knew that I needed to be very careful about letting too much negativity into my mind. I knew Satan would use it to try and overwhelm me with fear. I'm not saying that I wanted to refuse the truth or stick my head in the sand in hopes that it would all go away. No, I was choosing to believe what God's Word says in Isaiah 53:5. That He, (Jesus), was wounded for our transgressions, he was bruised for our iniquity. The chastisement for our peace was upon him, and by his stripes we are healed! I refused to give the devil any ammunition to assault me.

After getting back home, I sent the second email to the Victory Team:

Hello again V-Team! First of all, thank you for joining in the fight with us! We are so so grateful!

We visited Dr. W. today & he believes current cancer is stage 3, (which is what it was thought to be at the time). I will have a complete MRI & Pet Scan next Friday, July 17 starting at 7am. So, between now & then there are several specific prayer targets that we are requesting:

1. No further spread occurs & what is there must RETREAT & BOW at the precious Holy Name of Jesus!

2. That supernaturally God infuses my body NOW with the HEALING VIRTUE of Jesus & healthy cells over take cancerous cells NOT vice-versa!!!!

3. That our ALMIGHTY GOD continues to cover us with HIS PEACE, which surpasses all understanding and guard our hearts and minds through Christ Jesus. Philippians 4:7 NKJV

He IS showing Himself so STRONG to us & we are humbled by His love & presence!

We love you all so very much & thankful for friends & family like YOU!

Rick & Pam

A few days later, Pam and I returned to the Shepherd's House. On the way up there, we stopped at my in-law's house. It was my father-in-law's birthday. My mother-in-law, Mary, is in her early eighties and was relatively healthy outside of some bouts with dementia that seemed to be getting worse. She was generally very quiet and often would appear lost when it was time to eat or go somewhere. It was tough on Pam watching her mom decline in this state.

After we had spent some time with them, they wanted to pray over me before Pam and I left their house. As we formed a circle and placed our arms around each other, something miraculous happened. All of a sudden, this little frail mom became another person. Like Samson in the Old Testament, Mary began to pray boldly over me! I will never forget it as long as I live. We were witnessing firsthand the supernatural power of God right before our eyes! It touched my heart as I heard her pray so forcefully in a spiritual language that I knew was interceding for me! As Pam and I walked out of their house that day, I turned to her and said, "You know we just witnessed a miracle don't you?" "Yes," she replied.

The night before the PET scan, I had been instructed to refrain from any sugar and carbohydrates. A specific diet was given to me regarding what I could and could not eat. Upon arrival, I was taken first for the MRI. After completing the brain scan, I was sent for the PET scan. The technician inserted a port in my arm where my sugar level was assessed. Then, she visited a room where the radioactive tracer, as they call it, is removed from a subzero canister. It was then inserted into the IV port. "Come over here and sit in the recliner, Mr. Creel. Watch the soothing music and images on the video screen and do not use your phone or move around, just relax." "Why?" I asked. "Because the tracer will go to where you are exerting energy, and we want it to dissipate evenly all over your body. This way it will show the cancer well." "Hmm," I thought, "They want to ensure that I don't have excess sugar in my body, and then they say this tracer will find the cancer and light it up." In the words of Forrest Gump, "I'm not a smart man," but it sounds to me like the cancer must be attracted to sugar. That may not be 100 percent accurate, but I truly believe too much sugar will work against you if you have cancer.

After about 45 minutes, the technician came back to where I was in the recliner. "Are you ready?" I replied that I was. Upon entering the room for the scan, there was a large machine similar to the CT scan but a little different. I was instructed to remove everything from my pockets and lie down on a very narrow table. My arms were strapped beside me so they wouldn't fall off the table during the scan. Much like the CT scan, the machine started to swirl around me, as I would make passes all the way through the tunnel to the other side. After making several passes through, the test was soon over. Gathering my belongings, I headed out the door to where Pam was waiting for me.

A lot of things go through one's mind as you receive a lung cancer diagnosis and then have to wait several days until you actually know the extent of the disease. One night before the results came in, Pam and I were lying in bed. "My neck is hurting," I said. "I feel pains going up my neck." "You don't think it's that cancer gone to your brain do you?" "I don't know," I told her. "Just pray for me," I said. And pray she did! As Pam began to pray, she soon began speaking in a bold heavenly language that I knew was the Holy Spirit praying! I went right off to sleep!

4 OUR PART AND GOD'S PART

The following Monday evening, Dr. J. called, as he was covering for Dr. W. "Mr. Creel," he said. "Dr. J. here. I'm filling in for Dr. W. while he's out this week. I have the results back from your MRI and PET scan. There is no cancer in your brain, none in your liver, kidneys or other major organs. We see the tumor in your lower left lung, some spots between the sixth and seventh rib on your left side, the swollen lymph nodes in the center of your chest, and a couple of spots behind your right collar bone. It's pretty much confined to your thorax area." After a few questions back and forth, I told Dr. J. that I was a Christian and that I was trusting the Lord through this. I also told him that I had changed my diet and stopped a lot of the sugar intake and had eliminated diet drinks. He supported the reduced sugar adjustment that we had made and let us know that we would see him on Wednesday to start chemotherapy.

I had determined that I was not going to go online and look up chemo treatment or how it would affect me. I did not want to predispose my mind to how I "was supposed to feel." I was praying and was also asking the Victory Team to help us pray that there would be NO side effects from these treatments in Jesus' name! Here's the next email that I sent:

Hello V-Team (Victory Team!!)

We just wanted to give everyone an update & some targets for your prayers. First of all, THANK YOU! THANK YOU! THANK YOU! For praying & standing with us! I have been praying for the Lord to return to you 100 fold for your kind efforts. By the way, is there anything we can pray about for you?

We heard from the oncologist today regarding the MRI & PET scan. No cancer in my brain or other places in my body other than my left lung, thorax area & a place above my right collarbone. We Praise the Lord for this report & believe that HE IS ALREADY AT WORK stopping, shrinking & eradicating the cancer! Also, please target my throat as I have had some difficulty swallowing.

I am supposed to meet with the Dr W.'s partner, Dr. J., on Wednesday to start treatment. Please pray for divine wisdom, supernatural insight & skill as they formulate a treatment plan.

I feel good, I'm not short of breath, walking regularly, and eating well. The Lord has been so FAITHFUL to our family as we are not walking in fear but TRULY have the PEACE of God standing guard over our hearts & minds, Phil 4:7. We are trusting Him completely for healing, as we know this battle has ALREADY BEEN WON & it is not our battle but the Lord's! We are simply holding His mighty hand tightly as He leads us daily every step of the way.

We love you all,

Rick & Pam

Pam and I started making many adjustments in our lives to position ourselves for victory. We were vigorously learning about a healthy diet, getting plenty of sleep, and most importantly, filling our minds with God's Word! One of the many lessons that I learned is there is always your part and God's part...He will not do yours and you cannot do His! Now don't misunderstand me, I'm not implying that we somehow earn God's favor and blessings; we can't. The complete work of salvation was done through Jesus' death on the cross. "For by grace you have been saved through faith, and that not of yourselves; it is the gift of God, not of works, lest anyone should boast," (Ephesians 2:8-9 NKJV). But when it comes to obeying God, the principle of our part and God's part is all throughout the Bible. Here are just a few Scriptures relating to this topic:

"If My people who are called by My name will humble themselves, and pray and seek My face, and turn from their wicked ways, then I will hear from heaven, and will forgive their sin and heal their land," (II Chronicles 7:14 NKJV).

"Bring all the tithes into the storehouse, that there may be food in My house, and try Me now in this," Says the LORD of hosts, "If I will not open for you the windows of heaven and pour out for you such blessing that there will not be room enough to receive it," (Malachi 3:10 NKJV).

"Draw near to God and He will draw near to you," (James 4:8a NKJV).

As you can clearly see from just three verses, much of what God does is contingent upon what we do. Something else I've learned about God regarding this...our part is always natural, meaning something we have the power to do. His part is supernatural! And last, but not least, our part is always first! All too often, we say things like, "I just wish the Lord would move in my situation" or, "I sure wish the Lord would give me a sign." We are often waiting on the Lord to move and He is waiting on us to move!

I guess my first real experience with something that clearly demonstrates this thought of "our part and God's part" was back in 1999. Pam and I had decided to build a house. We had decided that we really couldn't afford to have the house that we wanted built by a general contractor, so we subcontracted the work ourselves. I had overseen many projects at work over the years and felt confident that we could do this. Let me pause right here and say—this is not for the faint of heart!

We were moving along quite nicely with the house when it was time to hire a brick mason. I really did not know any people in that field so I got a recommendation from a coworker. Well, being the optimist that I am, I didn't really check out his work at all and just assumed that he would do an excellent job. As you will see, I soon figured out how wrong I was!

At the end of the first day when I drove onto the property, I noticed some uneven bricks. Wanting to believe this person was going to work out, I told myself that these bricks were just coming up out of the foundation and would be covered with fill dirt. However, I did call the man that night and questioned him about his work quality. The conversation went something like this, "Mr. Taylor (not his real name), I don't really know you but I noticed some uneven brick when I inspected your work today. I just want you to know that your work needs to improve going forward." Now, in retrospect, I should have known right then and there that if this is how he performed on his first day on the job, nothing good could follow.

As the next few days went by, things got worse. Finally, on day four, I drove up, and the bricks were clearly above the foundation level. They looked awful! I could no longer stand it

27

anymore, nor could I talk myself into tolerating this man's work any longer! Something had to be done now! I called him on the phone almost immediately and told him that this was not going to work out. I asked what I owed him and he said he would be there in the morning to pick up his things.

Pam and I, along with some friends of ours, spent the next several hours pulling the brick off of the house before the mortar set. We pulled hundreds of the brick off until it was breaking the skin on my hands! What a night!

In the days before that occurred, I remember just agonizing over this whole ordeal. In retrospect, here is what I learned. First, I should have checked out some of this man's work before I hired him. Second, when I saw the poor quality continue even after I had talked to him about our expectations, I should have stopped it. I'm sure I probably prayed and talked myself into believing it was all going to work out—when clearly it was not! You see, I had the power to stop this at any time rather than let it continue. I just didn't want to confront the issue! The Lord wasn't going to stop the man when it was in my control to do something about it. In other words, this was my part to do. Here's a very important life lesson: we can't complain about what we allow. You see, there are times in life when we want the Lord to "fix" something that we have the power and control over. Sometimes it's a bad habit or being over weight. There is a part we play in doing something about it. I am not saying the Lord won't help us, because He will. But He WON'T DO IT ALL FOR US! I could have prayed until I was blue in the face, and guess what? I would have a house with crooked, uneven brick all over it!

So, back to our story. Pam and I watched videos about healthy foods to eat and foods to avoid. We learned that in general, the American diet is NOT GOOD! Americans consume too many sugary sodas, unhealthy diet drinks full of sugar substitutes, too much meat filled with hormones, antibiotics, and all kinds of chemicals, most of which we can't even pronounce. If you doubt what I'm saying, start reading the ingredients on something as simple as breads or a box of crackers!

We wanted to position ourselves for the best opportunity to succeed. I believe the Lord was guiding us every step of the way. The weight dropped off as I was about 206 and within about three weeks, I was down about 20 lbs. I lost even more as time went on, and while I'm sure part of it was the chemo, most was related to no longer consuming a lot of sugar! I also purchased a wonderful book entitled *Anti-Cancer* by David Servan-Schreiber. This resource is filled with so much information to help live a healthier life.

On Wednesday of that week, I went in for my very first chemo treatment. The lab technician inserted an IV port in my arm and took some blood samples before sending me to see the oncologist. After visiting with him for several minutes, I was sent to the infusion room. As I entered the half-round portion of the building full of partitions and recliners, I soon was led to a recliner with an IV pump that would be my resting place for the next two to three hours. The entire drug regimen was explained. Documents explaining the side effects of each one were also given to me. Then, the first IV bag was administered. Then the second. Then an anti-nausea med. Then, another bag. Finally, the last one was given and followed by a B-12 shot. They said, "You're all done, Mr. Creel! Call us if you have any problems. Do you have your next appointment?"

On the way home, I was somewhat emotional, having a little pity party I guess. I had heard what chemotherapy did to people—severe nausea, throwing up, diarrhea, severe fatigue. "How will I keep my spirits up if this happens to me," I thought. Visions of seeing myself lying lifeless in the bed, suffering from the effects of these drugs would sometimes flash through my mind. I learned to not dwell on that nor fill my mind with what was "supposed to happen to me." I prayed and asked others to do the same. I was given three levels of nausea meds to counteract the after-effects if needed. I was instructed to try the first one, and if no relief came, move quickly to the second. Finally, if nothing worked, go to the third one. I was instructed to do this at the first hint of any nausea, as they did not want me to get in a downward spiral. The next day I sent an email update to the V-Team:

V-Team Update

Hello all....I hope that you are having a wonderful week.

I just wanted to fill you in on the latest. I had the first round of treatments yesterday. All went extremely well & I thank the Lord for that!

Here are some things I would like for you to join us in prayer about over the next several weeks. First, allow me to give just a quick explanation of how these drugs are designed to work, (at least how I understand it). Cancerous cells have no checks & balances like healthy cells, they are radical & chaotic cells that constantly try to replicate. This is how the chemo identifies them, targets them & destroys them. The only issue is the drugs don't know the difference between cancerous cells replicating & healthy cells replicating. That is why there are side effects as good cells also are destroyed. So, here's the prayer strategy:

Ask the Lord to cover & protect all healthy cells with His precious blood & healing stripes. Just like the blood was placed on the doorposts of the Israelites to cause the death angel to pass over, let the healthy cells have that protection!

Since we are asking the Lord to target ONLY the cancerous cells, We Declare IN THE NAME OF JESUS that the cancerous cells be destroyed at an exponential & unprecedented rate!

That the immunotherapy join with my immune system, building an army of antibodies to ALSO DESTROY EVERY cancer cell IN JESUS GREAT NAME!

Finally, agree with us that this medicine will have NO adverse effects on me and that my body, strength, and appetite remain steadfast & STRONG in Jesus' name! And that the doctors, nurses & staff will be astounded at the MIRACLE-WORKING POWER OF GOD, to which WE GIVE HIM ALL THE GLORY & PRAISE!!!!!!

Thank you all so much for joining with us! I know that your prayers are making a tremendous difference & we are SO GRATEFUL!

We love you all,
Rick & Pam

Over the next few days, I noticed some fatigue, especially if I worked outside in the heat doing something strenuous. I also noticed some nausea about the third or fourth day in. However, it was nothing like what I thought it might be. I would pretty much make myself eat. I was eating mostly a plant-based diet of oatmeal with blueberries, strawberries and raspberries for breakfast. I ate tuna fish for lunch or, occasionally, a peanut butter and jelly sandwich. Of course, the jelly was low sugar. I read every label on just about everything I ate. I was looking for two things primarily: how much sugar was in it and if it had phosphate. I found out that phosphates are in many foods as a preservative that increases shelf life. However, in my research, I found out that a study was completed with mice that had been injected with lung cancer. Two groups of mice were fed over the course of a few weeks. One group was given the normal American foods, (which consisted of foods rich in phosphates). The second group was fed healthier foods without phosphates. Tumor growth was much greater in those fed the phosphate diet. Once I found out about the phosphates, I paid very close attention to what I was consuming. [1]

One morning I got up to prepare my coffee as usual. In preparing my coffee, I had ALWAYS added a lot of nondairy creamer. On that particular morning, I picked up the container and read the ingredients....PHOSPHATES! Wow, I had been adding lots of that for many years! That stopped immediately! Sure, my coffee did not taste the same, and I had to find a substitute. I started adding unsweetened soymilk. The coffee didn't taste quite the same, but it was close enough.

I was to return to the cancer center every three weeks to continue this regimen. After four rounds, I was to be scanned again. I was making significant diet changes, trying my best to minimize or eliminate preservatives, not eating hardly any dairy or meat with the exception of fish. I ate no sweets, no sodas, no diet or sugar free foods. I went from 206 down to 180 in a matter of four or five weeks. I still ate as much as I wanted except it was mostly plant-based. For snacks, I would eat nuts or fruit. If I wanted a bowl of cereal, I ate whole grain with nuts and oats and soymilk. Dr. W. didn't have much to say about my diet, but one time when I told him that I was eating a mostly plant-based diet, he said, "You're making my job easy."

There were highs and lows along the way for sure. However, I was very optimistic and faith-filled as I made it a point to read my Bible almost daily, then go on a walk and pray. One weekend, not long after I received the diagnosis, one of my friends, who is also a doctor, texted me. He said he had felt impressed to share something with me. Here's the essence of that text: "In the book of Exodus, Moses was leading the Jewish nation across the desert as Pharaoh was in hot pursuit. Finally, they found

[1] Coffey, Stella. 2011. "Anticancer: A New Way of Life, 2nd Edition. By David Servan-Schreiber. 2009. Viking Penguin, London. ISBN 978-0-670-02164-2." Renewable Agriculture and Food Systems 26, no. 1: 92–93. https://doi.org/10.1017/S174217051000058X.

themselves with the Red Sea at their back and Pharaoh closing in. I believe you may have similar feelings. I doubt that any of the million-plus Jews were thinking that the next morning that God would prepare a dry path for them through the Red Sea. I think sometimes we put human limitations on God. He has solutions to problems we have never considered. The Bible clearly says that our thoughts and our ways are not His ways. I know that I don't think like God. I do believe that God only asks us to trust in His decisions and purposes even when we are confused. We are praying for you and your family. Continue to put your trust in God's plans. Who knows—a path may open up across your Red Sea."

The same weekend another dear friend of ours sent me the following text: "One time when I was praying for mother and thinking about her healing, (her mom had liver cancer), a sentence came to me....it was 'my healing is limited to your parameters.' I had to look it up and read the meaning of parameters before I could even figure out what this meant. Healing is limited by the boundaries I, (humans), set based on our thinking."

Then later that day, the title of the Sunday message was "Don't Box Me In." Our immediate family happened to be at the Shepherd's House that particular weekend, and we had watched our church service online. After the message, I told our family that I believed the Lord was telling us something through all of this. This is the message: allow the Lord to heal me and work however He wants to do it. I need to try not to confine Him to our time tables and ideas, but let Him be who He is!

5 MY GOD IS STRONG

Over the next week or so, my son and daughter-in-love, (as we call her), wrote a song for us. They are both very talented in music and worship. They came over and sang it for us one night. Pam recorded the song from her phone as they sang, and it became our anthem of strength over the next several months! Here's the title and words captured in the next V-Team email update:

I just wanted to give you an update on things. As you know I had the first round of treatments a week & a half ago, Wednesday, July 22nd. The remaining treatments will occur every three weeks. This will put the last treatment ending September 30th. Then another PET scan will be scheduled.

I have experienced very few issues with the chemo; occasional fatigue & some very minor nausea, as I was instructed to rest & take the prescribed nausea medicine at the first hint. I am maintaining normalcy & continue to work from home. I feel really well & don't experience ANY pain. The Lord has been especially GOOD TO ME!

Prayer targets for the coming weeks:

That my throat will be healed as I still have trouble swallowing.

That adenocarcinoma MUST CONTINUE TO BOW & be evicted (as it is trespassing the temple of the Holy Spirit) in the NAME of JESUS!!!

Stone & Hayden have written a song that they shared with us this past week. I can't wait for you to hear it! In the meantime, here are the words:

Verse

Though I walk through the valley

And darkness surrounds me

I am not afraid

I'm on my knees crying out

Chorus

My God is strong

He knows all my needs

My God is strong

I don't have to worry

My God heals

There's not a battle He hasn't won

He's on the throne

My Prince of peace.

Verse 2

The enemy

Whispers lies to me
Of death & despair
But Jesus
Brought us healing
And life abundantly

Chorus
My God is strong
He knows all my needs
My God is strong
I don't have to worry
My God heals
There's not a battle He hasn't won
He's on the throne
My Prince of peace.

Bridge
My banner
My peace
My Shepherd
My Victory
Everlasting
My Provider
He is Righteous
The One who sanctifies us
My Healer
Redeemer

Chorus
My God is strong
He knows all my needs
My God is strong
I don't have to worry
My God heals
There's not a battle He hasn't won
He's on the throne
My Prince of peace.

It has blessed us so many times already.

Please let us know if there is anything we can pray with you about. I pray God's richest blessings on you all & thank you for standing with us!

We love you all,
Rick & Pam

    Pam and I would lie in bed at night listening to that song and those words and just cry, as we knew the Lord had given them that song just for us! I would like to tell you that things began to improve immediately, but in truth, things got worse!

    By now, the swollen lymph nodes in my chest were pressing hard against my esophagus, which was causing my food to back up. When I would eat, I would have to eat slowly, take small bites, and drink almost after every bite. Twice I choked and had to run over to the sink and cough out what I had swallowed as it had backed up in my throat. It was not pleasant at all, and it was so painful to know that my family was watching me, wondering just how bad this was going to get. I have never eaten slowly, which is probably a bad trait. However, it was getting to the place where I was the last one to finish my meal. It would have been easy to panic as bite after bite of food seemed to barely go down. However, the Lord helped me tremendously and I would not allow myself to dwell on the "what if's"! He is so faithful!

Twice a year our church always has 21 days of prayer. In January of each year, we have 21 days of prayer and fasting. In August, (strategically scheduled for just before harvest season), we have our second 21 days of prayer. It was during the August prayer period that I was getting up at 6am, going out on the deck to watch the prayer services online. Our wonderful Pastor, Chris Hodges, was using some prerecorded video devotions from various pastors and leaders as part of the morning services. On one particular morning, a minister talked about the Bible story of Peter walking on the water. Even though I had heard the story many times, there was something different about this devotion. The minister said it like this: "Peter was able to walk on top of what most people sink into and drown in because he had his eyes on Jesus!" Wow, I thought, I have had such peace as we have encountered the trial we're facing. Our faith was strong and we had been confident the Lord was at work. Now to hear this little devotion that morning was confirming why we had been so victorious...we were literally walking on top of a diagnosis that so many fall prey to and feel helpless toward because we were keeping our eyes on Jesus. Let me stop here and say that I do not profess to understand why some people are healed and others are not; I don't know the answer to that question. I would never try to say someone is weak or even imply that might be the reason they were not healed. Everyone is different. I would never try to put myself in another's place. I am me, and all I know is my situation and what we did to depend on God.

As I thought about the devotion that morning and how Peter was able to miraculously overcome the physics of nature as long as he kept his eyes on Jesus, I asked the Lord this question: "How do I keep my eyes on You when the wind is howling and the lightening is flashing?" He quickly responded to me with these words, "You worship Me." In the coming days and even now, we don't watch TV as we did before. We watch worship videos on YouTube. Wow, what a nightly—and sometimes daily—infusion of God's Holy Spirit this would bring to us! Sometimes during the day, doubt would try to enter and attempt to erode my faith. These nightly sessions would empower us again with new life and renewed faith to trust the Lord.

Not only were we changing our diet of natural food, we were also changing our diet of spiritual food. Pam set her clock alarm to awaken at 4am morning after morning to pray for me. I remember asking her if she wanted me to get up as well. She told me, "No, this is my battle." Later she told me that she had started getting up at 5am to pray but felt this was not the right time. So, she started getting up at 4am. I later found out through studying my Bible that the number four means "the door." Pam was going to the door each morning and knocking on it! This gave me such confidence to know the sacrifice she was making and how I knew the Lord was hearing her!

As I have said, I was experiencing four symptoms that had been getting worse: the relentless cough, the wheezing, trouble swallowing my food, and coughing up blood. One Saturday morning at the Shepherd's House, we were having breakfast with our family. After breakfast my son Stone said, "Boy, dad, you wolfed that down like it was nothing!" I replied, "You know, Stone, I didn't even think about it!" But he was right. I had just eaten a whole meal and never given it a thought! The swallowing WAS getting better! Thank You, Jesus!

It was soon time for the second round of chemo. Again, to keep those updated who were praying for us, I sent out the following:

Good afternoon Victory Team! I'm currently having my second round of treatments as I write this email. I feel very well & continue to do all things normal except wearing a mask & getting to go to the store every time I would like to. But I'm not complaining...the Lord has been too good for that!

I know I've said it before but I will never be able to thank you all enough for the prayers & support that you have given. Pam & I are forever grateful & pray God's gracious favor & manifold blessings upon you! I know that was too many "&'s" in a sentence...Pam will just have to ignore my grammar.

The Lord is using this season to do some incredible things that hopefully, I can share at some point. Stone is finalizing the song he & Hayden have written & wants me to play bass & his mom to play keys on it. More to come on that.

Finally, the prayer targets:

1. The chemo to DESTROY only the cancerous cells with no side effects.

2. The immunotherapy to FORTIFY my immune system & OVERTAKE the cancerous cells.

3. My throat to continue to improve & be UNRESTRICTED in any way.

My body is the Temple of the Holy Spirit, my heart has the blood of Jesus applied to it, therefore this cancer cannot reside in the SAME PLACE...adenocarcinoma must bow & LEAVE in Jesus Great Name!!!! Things Change When We Call Your Name!!!

We love you all so very much,
Rick & Pam

My friend David Anderson had sent me a text along the way telling me that "things change when we call your name." Not knowing exactly what he was talking about, I asked, "Is that a song?" "Oh yes," he replied and then promptly sent the link to Todd Dulaney's "Your Great Name." Wow, what a song! These are the songs, texts, words and so many encouragements that we kept near and dear to our heart that would get us through on the dark days and keep us encouraged on the good days.

I wish I could tell you that every day was awesome and I was able to breeze through without any concerns. However, that wasn't the case. I remember one day that we stopped at a store and Pam went in to get a few things while I sat outside in the car. While I was sitting in the parking lot, I saw two ladies come out of the store pushing a buggy filled about halfway with nothing but bottles of soda! I don't remember seeing anything else in their shopping cart! Not only that, they were overweight. I remember thinking, "Why do I have cancer and they don't?" They were obviously not being good stewards of their bodies. However, we have to know that as Christians, part of the tests we face can often involve the temptation to become bitter and blame God for our issues. We can start to compare ourselves with others and start asking questions like "why is this happening to me? I haven't done anything wrong, I'm not abusing my body. I go to church, I pay my tithes—this isn't supposed to be happening to me!" But I have to remind myself of a few things. Jesus wasn't crucified because of what He did wrong. Jesus was crucified because of what He did right! We may say that God will deliver, heal, provide and give us peace when we're afraid. But until we have been faced with these issues, we really can't speak from experience. I don't know about you, but I have a whole lot more interest in listening to someone that has experienced life's difficulties versus someone that describes them based on research or something they have read about. As the old saying goes, there can be no testimony without a *test*! Rest assured that if we profess Christianity, we will face tests in life designed to prove it!

I have been a student of God's Word for many years. I started teaching Sunday School when I was in my early twenties. For some thirty plus years I have studied and prepared countless Bible lessons. It has been one of my greatest joys to study and learn the life lessons of the Bible. I have a Hebrew-Greek study Bible that I cherish. I do word studies of the Hebrew and Greek words, the languages of the original Old and New Testament. One of the many revelations that the Lord gave me while going through this season was from James 1, verses 2-4; "My brethren, count it all joy when you fall into various trials, knowing that the testing of your faith produces patience. But let patience have its perfect work, that you may be perfect and complete, lacking nothing." In my word studies, I discovered the following: there are two types of trials or tests. God will prove our faith and satan will tempt us to fail. God will never tempt us, but our faith will be tested or "proved," as seen in I Peter 1:7. Here is what I believe the Lord showed me, (my paraphrase): My brother, count it as exuberant joy and excitement, when the Lord chooses to prove your faith. Knowing and understanding this, that the proving of your faith reveals the ability to refuse to surrender or succumb. Then, that refusal to give up will produce in you maturity, which helps us attain the goal(s) set by God that align with our calling and abilities. God desires that we be perfect and entire having all of the necessary equipment, lacking none!

Much like forged steel or gold purified in the furnace, our faith is only a word that we say until it has been tested! It's true—God is more concerned about our character than He is our comfort! The Bible clearly tells us in II Corinthians 3:18, "But we all, with unveiled face, beholding as in a mirror the glory of the Lord, are being transformed into the same image from glory to glory, just as by the Spirit of the Lord." The words "glory to glory" are from the Greek word "metamorphoo," where we get our word "metamorphosis." It's the caterpillar changing into the butterfly. The whole idea is God is maturing us, equipping us, preparing us. Why? So we can be more effective for Him!

I recently heard one of the best stories to demonstrate this truth. A bee keeper was explaining how the young bees are developed from the larvae. The bees place just enough honey in the hexagon cones where the larvae are placed for the young bees to develop and feed on until it is time to come out of the wax-sealed cell. When the honey runs out, the young bees have to bore a hole through the wax to get out. As they squeeze through the tight hole, something happens along the way that they don't realize until they escape. The membrane that has covered them is stripped away and a pair of wings are revealed! But the story isn't over. The bee keeper also explained that a moth once accessed the hive and ate the wax away from the larvae filled cells. When it was time for the larvae to hatch, there was no struggle to get out. Therefore, no wings were revealed and functional. Upon easily escaping, these young, flightless bees were soon stung to death!

The Bible says that the "thief does not come except to steal, and to kill, and to destroy. I have come that they may have life, and that they may have it more abundantly," (John 10:10 NKJV). I knew that the enemy of my soul was attacking my health. The Bible is clear about "who" brought sin and disease into this world. The Bible is also very clear about "Who" defeated sin and disease; "But He was wounded for our transgressions, He was bruised for our iniquities; The chastisement for our peace was upon Him, And by His stripes we are healed," (Isaiah 53:5 NKJV). In another place, the Bible tells us "how God anointed Jesus of Nazareth with the Holy Spirit and with power, who went about doing good and healing all who were oppressed by the devil, for God was with Him," (Acts 10:38 NKJV). The Bible is comprised of the Words of God. I want you to think about that for a minute. The Words of God!!!! It is impossible for God to lie. Heaven and earth will pass away but God's Word will NEVER pass away!!! I say this to remind folks that satan must bow to every Word that comes out of God's mouth!

To once again reference the story of Peter walking on the water, I want to point out something that the Lord reminded me of regarding that story. One of the most disturbing symptoms associated with adenocarcinoma was the fact I would cough up blood. As we all know, this is something very unnatural and unnerving to say the least. I know that the enemy of my soul was attempting to distract me and get my eyes off of Jesus by trying to get me to focus on these very disturbing and scary symptoms. After the second round of chemo, I started to cough up more blood! I remember the Lord telling me, "These are just symptoms,"—like the wind and waves of the storm that Peter was walking on top of —designed to get my eyes off of Jesus! I had to really work hard at reminding myself of this! However, one day I came back into the house after taking my walk. I sat down at the table and Pam asked me what was wrong. I know I was clearly distraught that day. As I was walking, I had coughed up a large amount of blood. Again, I didn't talk about symptoms, complain, or give hardly ANY attention to them. But this episode was hard to ignore.

When I explained to Pam what had happened to me she immediately went straight to the refrigerator and took out some grape juice and brought some crackers to the table. She begin to tell me about a text that one of her friends had sent her that morning. It was a story about about a lady that had been bitten on her leg by a brown recluse spider. After about a day or so her leg was red and swollen. All of her family members were telling her that she needed to see a doctor immediately! She said that night her leg was so swollen and red streaks were starting to go up her leg. The lady said, "I would not tell people to do what I did." (She was not advocating to refuse medical care.) But she said, "I said to the Lord, 'You've go to do something!'" She explained that the Lord told her to take communion. She did. The next morning her leg was completely healed!

That day we started taking communion at lunch time and continued for many weeks following. When we take communion, we become one with Jesus. We are partaking of His broken body, (the bread), beaten and stricken for our healing and peace. We take the juice, representing His blood poured out for our sins. That day was the start of some of the most powerful and precious times we had experienced throughout this entire ordeal. And guess what? Yes, not many days afterward, the coughing up blood minimized and then stopped completely!

Here is the email that was sent around that time:

Good Afternoon Victory Team...

I wanted to give you all an update of the latest news.

As I said last time my throat & swallowing is better and CONTINUES TO IMPROVE! I have also had this wheeze for the last few months that was getting worse. Guess what?? It is also practically GONE!!! And finally....YES the cough is also IMPROVING EVERY DAY!!! We are literally seeing the Lord heal my body right before our eyes!!

I want to thank you all for your prayers...WE ARE SEEING & EXPERIENCING the RESULTS!! Please continue to pray for:

Cancer to be completely gone in Jesus' name! "But He was wounded for our transgressions, He was bruised for our iniquities; The chastisement for our peace was upon Him, And by His stripes we are healed." Isaiah 53:5 NKJV

Dr. W. & staff to have supernatural insight & wisdom in caring for me.

The coughing to become NONEXISTENT! "No weapon formed against you shall prosper, And every tongue which rises against you in judgment You shall condemn. This is the heritage of the servants of the LORD, And their righteousness is from Me," Says the LORD." Isaiah 54:17 NKJV

I want to leave you with a little devotion Darius Daniels gave during our 21 days of prayer. He spoke about Jesus walking on the water & Peter also getting out of the boat to walk on the water toward Jesus in the middle of a storm. Peter was able to "walk on top of what most people sink into & drown in as long as he kept his eyes on Jesus!" The Lord, through HIS great mercy, kindness, & peace will allow us to walk on top of things in life as long as we KEEP OUR EYES ON JESUS!!! I asked the Lord "how do I keep my eyes on you?" & He quickly responded to me by telling me to Worship! Worship is how we keep our eyes on Jesus in the middle of life's storms!!! I can TRULY TESTIFY TO YOU ALL THAT THE LORD IS FAITHFUL!!!! Worship Him throughout your day & just WATCH WHAT HE WILL DO!!!

We love you all so much,

Rick & Pam

6 THE STATUS QUO WON'T DO

When I was in my late twenties and early thirties, I became hungry for more in life. I remember reading and listening to several of John Maxwell's leadership books and talks. He challenged me to be more, igniting something inside of me that I'm not sure that I can fully explain. As a young man, I had gotten a job right out of high school making $4.00 per hour. I worked hard and saved my money. In three months, I bought my first car and paid cash for it! As new opportunities were presented, I would bid on them. Within a short period of time, I was making the highest hourly wage in our plant. I went through the apprenticeship program and soon became a Journeyman Lithographic Press Operator. Not too long after that, I advanced into management. Eventually, I went from being a general laborer making $4.00/hr to becoming the plant manager. You hear stories like this from time to time, but I'm telling you I was literally that guy!

When I was about 40 years old, I was sitting on the front row of the church that we attended at the time. We had a visiting evangelist preaching that morning. Right in the middle of his message that Sunday morning, he stopped preaching, looked at me and asked me to come forward. I will never forget what happened next. He began to prophesy over me. He said, "The status quo will no longer do for you. I am going to take you to a place that when

I'm done, you will know that it was My hand that placed you there and not another." I wasn't sure what all that meant. Nevertheless, I have kept those words in my heart all these years.

In the last few years, I have prayed a prayer that goes something like this: "Lord, I want to give You everything I am. I want You to squeeze every drop out of my life and the resources that You have given me—so much so, that You will have to go down the hall in heaven and take some resources from someone else who didn't use all of theirs so I could have what I need to use for You!" As odd as this may sound, I believe that the Lord used this diagnosis to do just that. I'm not saying the Lord gave me cancer; He didn't. But He will use it for my good and to further His kingdom.

I was continuing the chemo every three weeks and coming up on round four. This email to our prayer team sums up how things were going at the time.

Hello Victory Team...

I hope everyone is having a great week. I just wanted to update you on progress to-date:

Trouble with swallowing is completely gone! Thank you Jesus!

Wheezing is completely gone! Thank you Jesus!!

The coughing is also improved as well.

We give ALL GLORY to God for what He has done & IS DOING!!!

When someone undergoes chemo it has an accumulative effect. So with each treatment white blood count takes a hit. My latest count put me barely above the "green light" threshold. However, it was so close that Dr. W. wanted to wait for this fourth treatment as he was concerned I would bottom out, (white blood count would get too low). So here are the latest prayer targets:

Pray that my white blood count goes up up up so the next round of chemo can occur in the next week.

That the coughing continues to improve & become nonexistent!

Finally, that the last cancer cell MUST surrender & exit this temple of the Holy Spirit. Also that the next scan reveal the miracle that we Are CONFIDENT & BELIEVE IS OCCURRING by the POWERFUL WORD of GOD!!!!!! Amen!!!!!!

Finally, for those of you that are on Instagram I have a new sight called dreams2destiny2020 where I post weekly devotional videos. If you have a chance check it out!

We love you all so VERY MUCH & will never be able to thank you enough for your support & prayers. Please let us know what we can pray about for you as well.

Rick & Pam

By the way, we were told that the insurance needed to approve the Neulasta shot that day to boost my white count. We asked about the cost. We were told it cost thousands! Pam and I went home that day asking the Lord to do what was needed. If we needed to wait a week for Him to move upon the insurance company to have them approve it, we would do it. This email sums up what happened the very next day!

Good morning Victory Team!!!

This is the day the Lord has made so let us REJOICE & be GLAD in it!

Good news...I was able to have the fourth treatment last Thursday, Sept. 24th. As you may recall my white blood count was borderline but Dr. W. recommended Neulasta which is an injection patch to boost my white count. However the insurance had to approve it. Pam & I went home that day simply praying "Lord, if we need to *wait a week for the count to come up or either allow the insurance to approve this patch". They called me the next morning, (Thursday), and said it is approved can you come today for treatment? By the way, they said the Neulasta cost several thousand $$$!! The Lord is so Faithful & True!!! That's His name you know in Revelation 19:11.*

They have scheduled a scan for me this coming Friday, October 9th. After the scan Dr. W. is going to bring my case up to the Doctor review meeting they have each Monday to discuss the plan moving forward. Then he wants to meet with Pam & me on the 15th. So, here are the prayer targets for this week:

That whatever is left, (if anything), of this defeated disease LEAVE THIS TEMPLE OF THE HOLY SPIRIT NOW & GO BACK TO THE PITS OF HELL FROM WHERE IT CAME IN THE ALMIGHTY NAME OF JESUS!!!!!!!!!!!!!!!!!!!!!!!!!

That a miraculous healing be revealed & confirmed by this scan that astounds the Doctors & staff so that ALL GLORY will go to Jehovah Rapha-"The God that Heals"!

That Dr. W. & staff have supernatural wisdom & Divine insight to know how to treat & direct us moving forward for an effective plan.

I know you may get tired of me saying this but I can't THANK YOU ALL ENOUGH for praying & standing with us in faith!! Many of you have texted or emailed us to encourage & send your personal support & it means so much to me. I am continuing to pray ABUNDANT BLESSINGS back on you all many times over!!!

We love you all & want you to know that YOU ARE PART OF THIS MIRACLE that God IS DOING,

Rick & Pam

I went in for the CT scan after four rounds of the chemo. This time was a little different, as I was instructed to drink some vanilla-flavored contrast—doesn't that sound appetizing? About 40 minutes prior to the scan, I remember that they put a straw in the bottle for me to sip. There was a lady in the waiting room that was watching me and gave me some advice: "I had several of those scans, so I'm telling you the best way to get that stuff down is just turn it up and chug-a-lug it!" That's exactly what I did! That was good advice and it made it so much easier!

After the results of the scan were in, we saw Dr. W for the report and the go-ahead to begin round five of chemo. Anxiously awaiting the report, Dr W. explained that about 50 percent of the cancer was gone. I was hoping for more—much more! Even though it was wonderful news that the cancer was being destroyed, I was disappointed. By the way, while I was initially diagnosed as stage III, Dr. W. had since changed the diagnosis to stage IV after he had seen the spread in the first PET scan.

Some other unexpected information was also shared on this visit. Dr W rolled his computer over in front of me. He showed me a graph. At first, I wasn't sure what I was looking at. But as he explained, it became clear. He was showing me a graph of the statistics of survival with this type of cancer. Pam was with me and saw it as well. I just sort of nodded as he explained what each line represented. It wasn't a very uplifting and positive experience. According to the stats, the odds were NOT IN MY FAVOR! I didn't want to see that graph. I didn't want to hear about those facts!

On the way home we didn't talk about the graph, the statistics, or what was discussed. However, once we got home, there was a heavy mental cloud hanging in the room. I was sitting at the kitchen table and said something like, "Pam, you know that graph that Dr. W. was showing us today?" That's all I had to say and I saw Pam immediately break down and cry. I got up and put my arms around her to embrace her as both of us were trying to process what we had seen that day. "I don't want to live without you," she said. "I know, Pam...but we are going to trust the Lord," I replied.

Over the next few days, I tried to stay positive and upbeat. I'm not going to lie: it was difficult. I would think to myself, *Why did Dr. W show me that graph? Why doesn't he try to encourage me?* He's a very good doctor, and I believe that he was just trying to prepare me and give the facts as best he could. A few days later, I woke up one morning and went out on the deck to have my devotion time with the Lord. Later that morning I wrote these words in my journal;

The last few days have been a little tough...doctors giving statistics, trends, and data. However, this is the arena that they operate in—facts, scientific data, and research. God does not operate in this earthly arena at all. God lives, moves, and operates in a supernatural dimension—a dimension ABOVE the natural realm. Numbers, data, statistics do not diminish one fraction of God's unlimited power and ability! The science and data may all be facts, but God's Word is the Truth. And the Truth is Always Greater than the facts! Truth > facts. As I awakened this morning ....those stats and facts were churning and turning inside my head trying to create fear and instability in me. I felt drawn to Psalm 91. Upon reading this Psalm a few verses stood out to me....verse 7, "a thousand shall fall at thy side and ten thousand at that right hand; but it shall not come nigh thee!" Verse 13, "Thou shalt tread upon the lion and the adder, (snake): the young lion and the dragon shalt thou trample under feet." Verses 14-16, "Because he has set his love upon Me, therefore I will deliver him; I will set him on high, because he has known My name. He shall call upon Me, and I will answer him; I will be with him in trouble; I will deliver him and honor him. With long life I will satisfy him, and show him My salvation."

After studying this Psalm, I opened the One Year Bible reading for that day and that Psalm was in the One Year Bible! There are 365 devotions in the One Year Bible—obviously one for every day of the year. What are the chances of me studying that Psalm on THE DAY it was there? I believe it was the Lord just confirming His Word to me that morning. It was overwhelming!

Little by little, I was witnessing the Almighty healing power of Jesus heal my body. As I already mentioned, the trouble swallowing and wheezing had completely disappeared, as well as the coughing up blood. It was amazing (and still is) to experience how the Lord miraculously healed me! I had also noticed considerable improvement in the nagging, persistent cough as well. One night, Pam and I were sitting in the family room and she said, "I haven't heard you cough today." I said, "It's getting way better, but I'm still coughing a little." She told me, "I'm waiting for the day when you don't cough at all!" Well, not many days later, that day finally came. After 18 months of nagging, relentless coughing, it was defeated and ceased. It, too, had to bow at the mighty name of Jesus!

At the beginning of January 2020, right after the very first procedure (the endoscopy), I had attended a prayer service during our church's 21 days of prayer. Of course, that was before I knew what was wrong with me other than the ongoing cough. I had gone down front and had a friend of mine anoint me with oil and lay his hands on me as the Bible instructs us in the book of James: "Is anyone among you sick? Let him call for the elders of the church, and let them pray over him, anointing him with oil in the name of the Lord. And the prayer of faith will save the sick, and the Lord will raise him up. And if he has committed sins, he will be forgiven," (James 5:14-15 NKJV).

Right after my friend prayed over me that day he leaned over and said, "Now I want you to text me when you stop coughing!" Well, guess what? I texted him in late November 2020:

I thought about something a little while ago...my cough is now completely gone. You told me to text you when it is gone. Well, here you go. Happy Thanksgiving!
"Is anyone among you sick? Let him call for the elders of the church, and let them pray over him, anointing him with oil in the name of the Lord. And the prayer of faith will save the sick, and the Lord will raise him up. And if he has committed sins, he will be forgiven."
James 5:14-15 NKJV

Man i am praying for you daily. I love seeing your updates and i know you are encouraging many thru this trial you are going thru. You are making a difference my friend - love and appreciate you

A little earlier that month I sent out an email to the Victory Prayer Team:

Good Morning Victory Team!!! This is the Day the Lord has made let us rejoice and be glad in it!! I like what Joyce Meyer says about expectancy...Every morning say "I'm expecting something good to happen to me today; I'm expecting something good to happen through me today; I'm excited about today and it's going to be a great day...I can't wait to see what it holds!" I'm a firm believer in the POWER OF OUR WORDS because the Bible tells us in Proverbs 18:21 "Death and life are in the power of the tongue, and those who love it will eat its fruit."

I have treatment #6 this coming Monday, November 23rd. By the way, Dr. W. said he has never given anyone six treatments of chemo...Is this not a testament to the POWER OF OUR LORD!!! I still have most of my hair, I don't feel like there is anything wrong with me, I eat like a pig, (I just try to eat well and avoid the bad stuff as much as possible). After this treatment I will have another scan on December 9th, and meet with Radiology, (Dr. E.), and then Dr. W. regarding treatment going forward. I believe with everything inside of me that the Lord is FAITHFUL TO HIS WORD and IS HEALING MY BODY. I read a declaration over myself every night...part of that declaration says "By the stripes laid upon the precious body of my savior, KING JESUS, ALL sickness is being eradicated as adenocarcinoma MUST BOW AND RETREAT at the Name of Jesus and by the POWER of HIS WORD...It is written in Isaiah 53:5 But He was wounded for our transgressions, He was bruised for our iniquities; The chastisement for our peace was upon Him, And by His stripes we are healed!!!!!!!!" Folks, I'm here to tell you that these are not just words written in some book long ago....NO, THESE ARE THE VERY WORDS OF GOD WHO CANNOT LIE AND REMAINS THE SAME FOREVER!!! I BELIEVE HE MEANT WHAT HE SAID AND SAID WHAT HE MEANT!!!!!

Prayer targets ahead:

1. That my body stay strong and well.

2. That Divine, supernatural wisdom, and supernatural innovation rest upon the Doctors and staff caring for me.

3. Finally, that the cancer continues to shrink until it is evaporated into nothing in the Mighty Name of Jesus!

Thank you again for your prayers and we pray MANIFOLD BLESSINGS BACK UPON YOU AND YOUR FAMILY!!

We love you all and are so grateful for your love to us!

Rick & Pam

7 PRAYING AND DECREEING GOD'S WORD

As I would take my morning walks, I would often recall to the Lord in prayer what He had done for me. I would say something like, "Lord, I am so grateful for how You're healing me. I remember just a few short months ago when I could barely swallow. I was wheezing, coughing, and spitting up blood. But little by little You healed me of every single symptom! Right before my eyes I saw it happen! There are NO WORDS to describe how grateful I am for what You have done!"

As I had stated in the last email to the prayer team, Dr W. hadn't ever given six rounds of full blown chemo to any of his patients before. But guess what? He gave #6 to me! The Lord had been so faithful to keep me strong and healthy just as we had prayed and asked Him! I had also learned about praying and declaring God's Word over myself. I had written a declaration in the notes on my phone and read this declaration over myself every night! The Bible says that "Heaven and earth will pass away, but My words will by no means pass away" (Matthew 24:35 NKJV). As I have already stated, God's Word is TRUE! When we speak God's words, we are repeating His covenanted promises that are ours because of our relationship with Him through the blood of His dear Son Jesus! On December 6, 2020, I sent this email out:

Hey Good Evening VICTORY TEAM!!! I know this email is being sent late this evening. I was going to wait until after our doctor visit on Wednesday before sending out another email but I felt impressed to send the email now.

Prayer and decreeing God's Word is how spiritual battles are won. God has given us His Word, we read it, hide it in our hearts, and decree it out of our mouths when we pray. "Death and Life are in the power of the tongue" Prov. 18:21.

I have witnessed four miracles that the Lord has performed right before my eyes concerning the symptoms that I was facing back in July and August. The coughing was the first symptom to show up many months ago that led me to pursue medical attention to begin with and the coughing has been the last symptom to leave...but IT HAS LEFT ME COMPLETELY!!! I have been coughing to some degree for over a year, BUT NOT ANY MORE!!!! ALL GLORY TO THE LORD FOR HIS WONDROUS WORKS!!!!

This Wednesday I have will have a CT scan that will determine the next steps. I have been careful to not try and dictate to the Lord "how" I should be healed, or try and fit Him into my time table and wish list. His ways are above my ways and His thoughts above my thoughts...God doesn't think outside the box...HE HAS NO BOX!! I submit myself to our UNLIMITED GOD TO WORK WITH HIS UNLIMITED POWER.

I'm more determined than ever to believe Him and stand on what He has said in His Word concerning healing and I know that you have been agreeing with us as well. I told someone not too long ago that I don't want to seek the healing but the HEALER. I've also come to realize something else over the last few months, the crucifixion of Jesus isn't just about forgiveness of sins, but also about taking away our grief, sorrows, our anxious thoughts, and healing our body, mind and spirit. Jesus' death, burial and resurrection represents the "Total Package" or as Pastor Larry Stockstill recently put it "Our Benefit Package".

I will end with this beautiful scripture in Isaiah 61; The Spirit of the Lord God is upon me; because the Lord hath anointed me to preach good tidings unto the meek; he hath sent me to bind up the brokenhearted, to proclaim liberty to the captives, and the opening of the prison to them that are bound; 2 To proclaim the acceptable year of the Lord, and the day of vengeance of our God; to comfort all that mourn; 3 To appoint unto them that mourn in Zion, to give unto them beauty for ashes, the oil of joy for mourning, the garment of praise for the spirit of heaviness; that they might be called trees of righteousness, the planting of the Lord, that he might be glorified.

YOU JUST CAN'T BEAT SERVING THE LORD!!!!

Thank you so much for your prayers and support...we love you all so very much,

Rick & Pam

The Word of God is our authority, our foundation, our confidence! His Word is sure! Like that old song says, "When all around is sinking sand, on Christ the solid rock I stand. When I need a shelter, when I need a friend, I go to the rock." When we pray, we are to come into agreement with His Word. We have His Word, the Bible. When we pray His Word, it is a powerful combination that is unstoppable!!! The enemy of our soul tries to get us to come into agreement with what he says: "You're not going to make it," or, "The odds are against you." The enemy says, "Look around, don't you see how many others didn't make it?" These are ALL lies fabricated to pull us away from what God says and create doubt and fear. That's why Jesus said over and over in Matthew 4, "It is written," because God's Word is the final authority! II Corinthians 10:4-5 says, "For the weapons of our warfare are not carnal but mighty in God for pulling down strongholds, casting down arguments and every high thing that exalts itself against the knowledge of God, bringing every thought into captivity to the obedience of Christ." The Word, the armor of God, the name of Jesus, the blood of Jesus, prayer, and worship are all POWERFUL weapons that the enemy can't stand against! He doesn't want us to know about them or use them! He wants us to listen to him and "reason" with him...that's a trick that he wants us all to fall for!

The Lord gave me a revelation while studying in Daniel chapter 3 about Shadrach, Meshach and Abed-Nego being thrown into the fiery furnace. The king, Nebuchadnezzar, had built a ninety-foot-tall image for all of his kingdom to worship. They would play music and all were to bow down to this image. However, Shadrach, Meshach and Abed-Nego did not comply with the decree. The king called them all into his presence and basically said something like this: "Maybe you guys didn't quite understand the rules. When the music plays, you are to bow down and worship the image. If you do not, I will have you thrown into a furnace and who can deliver you from my hands. Do you understand? We're going to try it again."

Here's their answer in Daniel 3: "Shadrach, Meshach, and Abed-Nego answered and said to the king, "O Nebuchadnezzar, we have no need to answer you in this matter. If that is the case, our God whom we serve is able to deliver us from the burning fiery furnace, and He will deliver us from your hand, O king. But if not, let it be known to you, O king, that we do not serve your gods, nor will we worship the gold image which you have set up," (Daniel 3:16-18 NKJV).

Here is the revelation that the Lord gave me regarding this story: just like Nebuchadnezzar erecting the ninety-foot-tall image, Satan erects strongholds that can loom large in our minds. By the way, the Bible tells us the image that Nebuchadnezzar built was six cubits wide and sixty cubits tall. Six is the number that represents "man." The word "image" in Hebrew means "attitude." There are certain words, such as "cancer," that have come to mean "automatic defeat." Satan tells us to bow down to it. The Hebrew is "nephal," or fall down, sink, succumb and decay. The music is played, (the diagnosis, the scientific facts, data, and statistics), and we're to bow down, give in, and comply. If we don't, we're going to face the consequences. Therefore, as verse 7 of Daniel chapter 3 says—at the appointed time, (seasons of life when a trial may come your way), the music plays, and EVERYONE is to bow down and worship the image. For those who don't worship these idols, the king says, "maybe you didn't hear me correctly...we're going to do this again." The music plays again and Satan whispers words like, "Didn't you hear the doctor say stage four cancer? Nobody escapes stage four!"

Can I just stop here and make a point? Shadrach, Meshach, and Abed-Nego didn't decide on that day what they would do. No, they made a commitment long before that day about Who they served! I heard someone say, "If you can't say 'no' to the king's meat (Daniel 1:8-15), you will never say 'no' to the king's idol!"

Back to the story. The king was so furious at their refusal to comply to his decree that he had the furnace heated seven times hotter than usual. It was so hot that two mighty servants were killed by the heat when they threw Shadrach, Meshach, and Abed-Nego into the fire! Notice the term "seven times." Seven is always the number for divine perfection and divine manifestation. Old Nebuchadnezzar didn't know it, but he was getting the furnace "just right" for the three Hebrew boys to get in!

The Bible tells us that when Nebuchadnezzar looked in the fire, he saw four men walking around and the fourth looked like the Son of Man. Jesus was in the fire with them! By the way, they were thrown in bound, but were set free in the fire! The fire of perfection burns stuff off of us and sets us free. Impurities float to the top in a fire seven times hotter. We're going to come through and come out purified—never the same! Why? Because we have been with Jesus! Those Hebrew boys came out unharmed, not a hair singed. And get this: there was not even the smell of smoke on their clothes—all while the audience looked on!

Early on, as I would take my morning walks, I would say to the Lord, "We're going to walk through this fire holding tightly to Your hand. We won't be harmed by this fire. And when we get to the other side we won't even have the smell of smoke on our clothes!" And speaking of the audience looking on, our friends would say things to us like, "Have you ever considered that y'all might be going through this so people like us can see how you handle this and learn from it?"

One last thing about the story. After it was all said and done at the end of Daniel chapter three, the king made a NEW decree. He knew "there is no God like the God of Shadrach, Meshach, and Abed-Nego." Afterward, the Hebrew boys were promoted by the king! You see, if we won't bow to the images of Satan, God will make the images bow to us by His power and faith in Him!

After the completion of the sixth round of chemotherapy, another CT scan was scheduled. As you can see from the email that I sent out, the Lord continued to show Himself strong!

Good morning Victory Team! I do have some victories to report today...CT scan last Wednesday has revealed CONTINUED HEALING and RETREAT OF THE CANCER! To sum it up, I am now ~70-75 percent cancer free!!! This, my friends, IS THE RESULT OF PRAYER and we are VERY GRATEFUL TO THE LORD FOR ALL HE IS DOING!! Dr. W. doesn't use many adjectives...he usually uses words like "good" and generally we don't get much more excitement from him than that. However, Wednesday he said that he was "thrilled" when he saw the latest scan!

Moving forward; I have met with Dr. E., (Radiologist), regarding radiation treatment for the remaining areas. There are four general areas that he plans to treat and we would greatly appreciate your continued prayer agreement with us to target all the points below:

1. Two faint spots behind my right collar bone that no longer show up on the scans but were on the original PET scan.

2. The lymph nodes in the center of my chest.

3. Two spots in my left lung between the 6th & 7th ribs.

4. A tumor in the bottom of my left lung where they believe this all originated.

Finally, that a SUCCESSFUL radiation plan be formulated to target ONLY THE CANCER CELLS. That I stay strong, healthy, AND my white blood count STAYS ELEVATED!

This scripture picture came to my mind while thinking about this email...in Exodus 17 as Israel fought the battle with Amalek, Moses went up to the top of a hill with the rod of God in his hand, (authority). When Moses held up his hand Israel PREVAILED! However, as the battle raged on Moses' hands became heavy and when he let down his hand, Amalek prevailed. So they put a stone under Moses so he could sit down and Aaron and Hur positioned themselves on one side and the other AND STEADIED HIS HANDS UNTIL THE GOING DOWN OF THE SUN...verse 13, So Joshua DEFEATED Amalek and his people with the EDGE OF THE SWORD!!! All of you have come along side of us and as you

*have joined with us in prayer YOU HAVE HELPED STEADY OUR
HANDS so that OUR GOD AND HIS WORD WILL PREVAIL!!!
This touches my heart even as I type this today....THANK YOU,
THANK YOU, THANK YOU for your support! WE GIVE GOD
ALL THE GLORY FOR THE THINGS HE HAS DONE, DOING,
and WILL DO!!! AMEN!!*

We love you all,
Rick & Pam

Shortly after the CT scan, I was scheduled to see the radiologist to set up radiation treatments. Dr. E., my radiologist, wanted me to have another PET scan and another MRI to ensure there was no cancer lurking in other places that may have been missed. They also wanted to gain a more precise picture of exactly where any cancer remained.

I have learned a few things about the different scans. A CT scan (computed tomography) basically shows where cancer may be located and defines some metrics. However, a PET scan (positron emission tomography) can actually measure the activity level of the cancer. SUV levels or standardized uptake values, are used to assign a numeric value to the activity level of the cancer. Obviously, the higher the value the greater the activity of the cancer.

After the second MRI and PET scan were completed, a nurse called me to say the tests didn't show any additional activity; she set up a date for me to come in for radiation prep. I really didn't think much more about it until Dr. E. called me the next week. "Mr. Creel, have your ears been burning this morning?" "Why is that?" I asked. "Dr. W. and I have been talking about you all morning! Nothing bad; it's good news!" Dr. E. went on to tell me that he was having trouble finding ANYTHING! "I had to go back to the original PET scan to even see where it was before! I see two places, but I could even make a case for it being gone! I showed this to one of my colleagues and they said, 'Wow, what kind of chemo did that guy have?' I told him just the regular kind like we give everyone else!" Dr. E. said that he was determined to not let the results of the scan change his course of action, but they were so compelling he wanted to call me and get my input.

Dr. E. continued to tell me that I have three options going forward: we could treat only the two places showing on the latest scan; we could treat all four spots that showed on the original scan; or we could forego the radiation and continue with the chemo. He also further explained the risks and benefits of radiation. "I burned a hole in a man's esophagus once. I also, punctured a man's lung. The long term effects can cause a rib to break under certain conditions. There's great risk but tremendous reward with radiation." I asked for some time to think about it and promised to call him the next day.

A few days later I sent this email to our Victory Prayer Team:

Hello wonderful Victory Team! I hope that you are all doing well. This morning I completed #5 of 15 radiation treatments. So far I have had no side effects & with your continued prayers activating God's abundant blessings, we are trusting that will continue in Jesus name!

I wanted to share a little story with you all to uplift your faith. Several days ago while talking to Dr. E., (radiologist) about the treatment options, I needed to give them an answer as to what option we wanted to pursue. Option 1) treat all four areas that showed up on the original PET scan, 2) treat only what was showing up now in the latest scan or 3) forego the radiation completely & move on to the maintenance chemo plan. Dr. E. explained the risks of the radiation but also the rewards. I told him that I would call him the next morning to let him know my answer.

Pam & I talked about it and we're leaning towards treating all four spots from the original scan.

That night everyone had gone to bed but me. As I sat in the den I began to pray and simply tell the Lord that He had been so faithful to lead us every step of the way & that I was confident that he would continue to lead us. I closed my eyes as I was praying & what happened next was nowhere in my thoughts. As I closed my eyes I saw the young shepherd boy David when he was gathering his stones to fight Goliath. And here's what I believe the Lord said to me, "you hurl the stone & I will make sure it hits the target." Then I heard myself pray these words "Lord, you are about to cut the head off of this giant!" The next morning I was up reading the One Year Bible before calling Dr. E. Pastor Larry Stockstill's devotion that day was about Israel being the Apple of God's Eye. He actually explained that this meant that Israel was the pupil of God's eye. He further explained that the pupil is what lets the light in, (radiation) but the eyelid FIERCELY PROTECTS the eye from damage! I believe the Lord was saying to me that "I will be your offense & your defense" through these two stories.

I called Dr. E. & told him to plan on treating all four places & do what he was trained to do because everything was going to be just fine! Folks I'm here to tell you that OUR GOD IS STRONG!!!

8 FROM THE ABUNDANCE OF THE HEART

During the radiation treatments, I would go in every morning to be treated. I didn't really elaborate on this in the prior chapter, but after the plan of treatment was developed, I had to have a wax mask made that covered my head and part of my shoulders. Since the treatment included the two original spots behind my right collar bone, this wax fixture held me perfectly still. Each morning, I would enter the treatment room and lie on a table while they would affix the wax mask fixture over my head and lock it into place. There were markings on the mask that allowed them to align the radiation beam precisely where it would hit the target. Then the mask was removed, and the technicians aligned the machine with the other markings they had placed on my body. In total, four targets were treated and this would take about 25 minutes each day.

I would lie as still as possible as I did not want to allow for any margin of error! The machine would make this loud buzzing sound when the radiation was turned on. The head of this large circular glass dish would rotate around me. As it would pass over, I could see a multitude of gray slots moving constantly. I knew this was targeting the radiation beams to perform as programmed. I didn't really know what to expect as far as side effects. They gave me some literature to read addressing the possibility of skin irritation and fatigue.

Every week I would meet with Dr E. and he would ask me how I was doing. My usual answer involved tiredness but nothing serious. I told him that I couldn't really tell that they were doing anything to me. I'm not sure if he thought I was being accusatory or not as on one occasion he said, "I can assure you that we are turning the machine on." After all fifteen rounds of the radiation were completed, I sent the following email to our prayer team:

Victorious Team!

It's been a little while since the last update so I wanted to tell you the latest. I just completed 15 rounds of radiation with little side effects....I know, these reports about "little to no side effects" sound crazy but I'm just telling you the TRUTH...It's just sounds too good to be true but it's NOT!

I read this out loud, over myself practically every night;

"Because he has set his love upon Me, therefore I will deliver him; I will set him on high, because he has known My name. He shall call upon Me, and I will answer him; I will be with him in trouble; I will deliver him and honor him. With long life I will satisfy him, And show him My salvation."

Psalms 91:14-16 NKJV

Would you just look at ALL THOSE "I wills"!!!! Why does He do all of this? Because we have SET our LOVE upon Him!!! The Hebrew word is "chashaq". When we SET our love upon Him we have DETERMINED to cleave to Him, delight in Him, He IS our life. Wow! Remember where He told us in His word to "Delight yourself also in the LORD, And He shall give you the desires of your heart." Psalms 37:4. Just like a loving parent wants their

children to live a rich & fulfilled life God wants the same for us!!!!
(I just had to teach a little right there...I can't help it!)

*Next step is to start maintenance chemo February 4th. This
consists of a lower dose for some period, (I don't know how long
yet), and I assume a follow up scan at some point. I will keep you
posted.*

*I can't tell you all how much I love you & we're SOOOOO
GRATEFUL for your prayers!!!!*

Rick & Pam

As mentioned in the last email, I developed and read a
declaration over myself nightly. As I said before, the Words of God
are the most powerful words that you can speak and declare over
yourself! Here is that declaration:

I believe that the Word of God, prayers, praise, and worship to my
God are going before me activating HEALING that is invading the
cancerous cells inside my body that are trespassing this Temple of
the Holy Spirit! I Corinthians 6:19 says: "Or do you not know that
your body is the temple of the Holy Spirit who is in you, whom
you have from God, and you are not your own? For you were
bought at a price; therefore glorify God in your body and in your
spirit, which are God's." By the stripes laid upon the precious body
of my Savior, KING JESUS, ALL sickness is being eradicated as
adenocarcinoma MUST BOW AND RETREAT at the Name of
Jesus and by the POWER of HIS WORD to COMPLETELY
DIMINISH INTO NOTHING, AND my white count increase and
stay up and creatinine go down; blood pressure BE normal in
Jesus' name. For it is written in Isaiah 53:5, "But He was wounded

for our transgressions, He was bruised for our iniquities; The chastisement for our peace was upon Him, And by His stripes we are healed." It is written, "Listen, all you of Judah and you inhabitants of Jerusalem, and you, King Jehoshaphat! Thus says the LORD to you: 'Do not be afraid nor dismayed because of this great multitude, for the battle is not yours, but God's," (2 Chronicles 20:15). I Peter 2:24 states "Who Himself bore our sins in His own body on the tree, that we, having died to sins, might live for righteousness— by whose stripes you were healed." So we declare and confess with our mouth that we hold tightly to Your Hand, Lord, as YOU LEAD US THROUGH the FIRE to the OTHER SIDE as written in Daniel 3:25-27. It is also written in Psalms 103:2-5, "Bless the LORD, O my soul, And forget not all His benefits: Who forgives all your iniquities, Who heals all your diseases, Who redeems your life from destruction, Who crowns you with lovingkindness and tender mercies, Who satisfies your mouth with good things, So that your youth is renewed like the eagle's." It is written in Psalm 91, "Because he has set his love upon Me, therefore I will deliver him; I will set him on high, because he has known My name. He shall call upon Me, and I will answer him; I will be with him in trouble; I will deliver him and honor him. With long life I will satisfy him, And show him My salvation." "The right hand of the LORD is exalted; The right hand of the LORD does valiantly. I shall not die, but live, And declare the works of the LORD," Psalms 118:16-17.

Along about this time my daughter, Carman was getting married. In June of 2020, just before I was diagnosed with lung cancer, her fiancé proposed to her at the Shepherd's House. Over the years, I watched her smile at different junctures of life. When she was just a young elementary student, she was involved in gymnastics and entered a meet with her team. She surprised us all by winning a medal in more than one event. I will never forget that smile on her face as she stood on the platform that day staring at her medal! I will also never forget the smile on her face when Dillon proposed...no words needed, the smile said it all!

She was so heartbroken upon hearing the terrible news that she asked Pam if she needed to move the wedding date up. She wanted her dad to be the one to walk her down the aisle. Well, guess what? On January 30, 2021, I did just that! She was the most beautiful bride ever! What a wonderful wedding with a full house of friends and family. The Lord certainly smiled down upon the Creel family that day as we celebrated Carman and Dillon's start of a new life together, and allowing me to be present and perform my fatherly role in the ceremony. What a great God we serve!

As February rolled around, one morning I was out on our deck having my devotion time with the Lord. When I read the One Year Bible for that day, Psalm 30:1-4 had this to say: "I will extol You, O LORD, for You have lifted me up, And have not let my foes rejoice over me. O LORD my God, I cried out to You, And You healed me. O LORD, You brought my soul up from the grave; You have kept me alive, that I should not go down to the pit. Sing praise to the LORD, you saints of His, And give thanks at the remembrance of His holy name."

As I read those words, I believe the Lord was speaking to me. It just hit me so powerfully and I started to cry as I thought about those verses! As of that morning there was a shift in my outlook. I'm not saying that I never had another negative thought about cancer, but there was a change. I told Pam about what had happened that morning as well.

Shortly thereafter, as I continued to read the nightly declaration, Pam asked me if I had considered changing my declaration. I told her that I had been thinking about it. I wanted to be careful that I was following the leading of the Lord and not just something that I wanted to do. Not too long afterwards I did change what I read nightly over myself to this:

It is written in Isaiah 53:5, "But He was wounded for our transgressions, He was bruised for our iniquities; The chastisement for our peace was upon Him, And by His stripes we are healed."

"I will extol You, O LORD, for You have lifted me up, And have not let my foes rejoice over me. O LORD my God, I cried out to You, And You healed me. O LORD, You brought my soul up from the grave; You have kept me alive, that I should not go down to the pit. Sing praise to the LORD, you saints of His, And give thanks at the remembrance of His holy name," (Ps 30:1-4).

Lord, I speak to my white blood count that it increase and stay up and that there would be NO pneumonitis in the authority of Jesus' name!

"Thus says the LORD, who makes a way in the sea And a path through the mighty waters, Who brings forth the chariot and horse, The army and the power (They shall lie down together, they shall not rise; They are extinguished, they are quenched like a wick): Do not remember the former things, Nor consider the things of old. Behold, I will do a new thing, Now it shall spring forth; Shall you not know it? I will even make a road in the wilderness And rivers in the desert," (Isaiah 43:16-19).

"For as the rain comes down, and the snow from heaven, And do not return there, But water the earth, And make it bring forth and bud, That it may give seed to the sower And bread to the eater, So shall My word be that goes forth from My mouth; It shall not return to Me void, But it shall accomplish what I please, And it shall prosper in the thing for which I sent it," (Isaiah 55:10-11 NKJV).

Lord, let these treatments do what they are ordered to do by You. Let there be NO adverse effects on me. I believe that you have ordered our steps by aligning us with Dr. W. and Dr. E. Let us fulfill our role in witnessing to them! Pam and I WILL SEE our greatest days in the latter part of our lives as John 2:10b says: "You have saved the best wine until NOW!" It is written in Psalm 91, "Because he has set his love upon Me, therefore I will deliver him;

I will set him on high, because he has known My name. He shall call upon Me, and I will answer him; I will be with him in trouble; I will deliver him and honor him. With long life I will satisfy him, And show him My salvation."

Amen!

As previously stated, I was scheduled to return to Dr. W. on February 4th to begin the maintenance chemo treatments. This consisted of one less chemo drug but continue for several months to ensure ALL cancer was gone. Upon returning to start these treatments, Dr. W. examined me and decided to wait a little longer before starting this regimen. There is a phenomenon that can occur when one of the immuno drugs is combined with radiation. This can cause pneumonitis, which is an inflammation of the lung tissue brought on by radiation therapy. As you may have noticed in the declaration I would pray nightly over myself, I would ask the Lord to "let there be NO pneumonitis in the authority of Jesus' name!" To be on the safe side, Dr. W. decided to wait another week and a half before resuming any treatment.

On Monday, February 15, 2021, I started the maintenance treatments. These treatments, like the others, would occur every three weeks. As the months and weeks passed, the Lord blessed me tremendously as I was able to tolerate these treatments very well. Yes, I had moments when the white count would take a dive and the Neulasta was needed to boost my white count. Also, occasional mild nausea was present, but thankfully nothing severe! The Lord kept me strong through it all!

Pam and I learned so much that I know we would not have learned any other way. Our lifestyle had changed. Many things had been pruned away from our lives. They weren't necessarily sinful things, just "things" that were preventing us from being our best. I heard Dr. Henry Cloud talk about pruning once. Dr. Cloud said that there are three times to prune: 1) When a rose bush has produced too many rose buds. The ones with the greatest potential are the ones left. 2) When a plant or a tree is sick and not getting well. The unproductive or unhealthy areas of our life must be dealt with, or they will eventually affect the healthy areas of our life. 3) When the limbs of a plant are dead and just taking up space. God is always calling us to a life of more. We will never experience more if we keep holding on to the past. Jesus said, "Remember Lot's wife."

We have some Crape Myrtle Trees that I prune almost every year. Those things grow so many limbs in one year that they become this tangled mess if they don't get regular pruning. Too many limbs feed too many small, insignificant avenues that end up just taking up space and energy. Isn't it the same with our lives? We get involved in too many things. If we don't have purpose and goals, we don't know what to say "yes" to and what to say "no" to. I heard Pastor Rick Warren say the word "no" is just as important as the word "yes." Some of us need to pay attention to that!

Not only are we to allow the Lord to prune away unnecessary things in our life, we're to also take possession of what is ours. Just like the children of Israel are instructed in Deuteronomy 7, we are to possess the land and drive out the enemy. After being in the wilderness for 40 years, (40 is a time of trial, 40 weeks-birthing something new), in verse 5 the Lord says "destroy" or "break the teeth, break down their groves and burn their graven images."

In the Old Testament, these were literal, physical battles that were symbolic of us fighting spiritual enemies today. They were to "utterly destroy them" as noted in verse 2. We are to make no covenant with them nor show mercy to them! Satan desires to deceive us by convincing us to coddle these things— immorality, sin, and yes, even sickness. Make no mistake, Satan is out to take you out! The Bible says in John 10:10 that "the thief comes but for to kill, steal, and destroy!" He has one goal and that is to prevent you from finding your purpose and doing what God has called us to do: "possess our land"!

Some might say, "You're too fanatical about all of this stuff; there is not a devil under every rock." Well, like my pastor says, "Maybe not every rock, but every other rock!" I'm convinced that if we are born again, faith-filled people of God, the devil will seek to destroy you! And He will seek to do that any way he can! But as the Bible teaches us, "Lest Satan should take advantage of us; for we are not ignorant of his devices," (II Corinthians 2:11 NKJV). Satan will take advantage of us to the degree that we are ignorant of his devices, schemes, and tactics.

We have to be able to recognize our enemies so we know how to fight and stand against them. If not, we may let them "live with us." Have you ever heard some one say "My diabetes is flaring up," or, "My cancer is stage 3." I realize that we can say these things unconsciously, but that's just it; be vigilant and don't own any sickness or disease.

Satan would like for our words to align with his doubts and fears. And if we're not vigilant, we can pray until we fall over and then turn right around and speak defeat! Have you ever heard this? "I've been praying about it, but I figured he would end up in the hospital." Our words must align with God's Word. And guess what? They will, if we will do what David said in Psalm 1, "Blessed is the man Who walks not in the counsel of the ungodly, Nor stands in the path of sinners, Nor sits in the seat of the scornful; But his delight is in the law of the LORD, And in His law he meditates day and night. He shall be like a tree Planted by the rivers of water, That brings forth its fruit in its season, Whose leaf also shall not wither; And whatever he does shall prosper," (Psalms 1:1-3 NKJV). The Bible tells us that from the "abundance of our heart the mouth speaks." What is in a person's heart? What comes out of their mouth. That's why we are to "hide His Word in our hearts that we might not sin against Him," (Psalm 119:11).

Not only must our words align with God, so must our actions. James 2:18 says, "But someone will say, 'You have faith, and I have works.' Show me your faith without your works, and I will show you my faith by my works." Very early on, I had to make a decision to NOT GIVE IN to the disease. I remember I was taking a shower right after being diagnosed with cancer. Afterward, I was getting ready to do what I had always done which is dry off the shower glass to help keep it clean. Right as I started to do this, a thought came to me, "Why are you doing this?" "What's the use?" I can tell you that if I had given in to that thought (which I believe was from the devil, by the way), I would have started down the road of defeat immediately!

Soon afterward, I listened to a sermon from Charlotte Gambill about the story of Mephibosheth in 2 Samuel chapters 4 and 9.

"Jonathan, Saul's son, had a son who was lame in his feet. He was five years old when the news about Saul and Jonathan came from Jezreel; and his nurse took him up and fled. And it happened, as she made haste to flee, that he fell and became lame. His name was Mephibosheth."

II Samuel 4:4 NKJV

"Now David said, 'Is there still anyone who is left of the house of Saul, that I may show him kindness for Jonathan's sake?' And there was a servant of the house of Saul whose name was Ziba. So when they had called him to David, the king said to him, 'Are you Ziba?' He said, 'At your service!' Then the king said, 'Is there not still someone of the house of Saul, to whom I may show the kindness of God?' And Ziba said to the king, 'There is still a son of Jonathan who is lame in his feet.' So the king said to him, 'Where is he?' And Ziba said to the king, 'Indeed he is in the house of Machir the son of Ammiel, in Lo Debar.' Then King David sent and brought him out of the house of Machir the son of Ammiel, from Lo Debar. Now when Mephibosheth the son of Jonathan, the son of Saul, had come to David, he fell on his face and prostrated himself. Then David said, 'Mephibosheth?' And he answered, 'Here is your servant!' So David said to him, 'Do not fear, for I will surely show you kindness for Jonathan your father's sake, and will restore to you all the land of Saul your grandfather; and you shall eat bread at my table continually.' Then he bowed himself, and said, 'What is your servant, that you should look upon such a dead dog as I?' And the king called to Ziba, Saul's servant, and said to him, 'I have given to your master's son all that belonged to Saul and to all his house. You therefore, and your sons and your servants, shall work the land for him, and you shall bring in the harvest, that your master's son may have food to eat. But Mephibosheth your master's son shall eat bread at my table always.' Now Ziba had fifteen sons and twenty servants. Then Ziba said to the king, 'According to all that my lord the king has commanded his servant, so will your servant do.' 'As for Mephibosheth,' said the king, 'he shall eat at my table like one of the king's sons.' Mephibosheth had a young son whose name was Micha. And all who dwelt in the house of Ziba were servants of Mephibosheth. So Mephibosheth dwelt in Jerusalem, for he ate continually at the king's table. And he was lame in both his feet."

II Samuel 9:1-13 NKJV

Mephibosheth was from Lo Debar which means "a dessert place" or "no pasture". He was lame in both feet. I certainly could identify with Lo Debar!!

Here are the three points that Charlotte Gambill made during her sermon that day:

1. Your current status does not alter your significance. God calls us by name not label.

2. Lo Debar may be your location but it's not your Destination....don't make PROVISION for Lo Debar! You WALK THROUGH the valley...you are never to stay there! We get through it with our attitude and confession. Lo Debar will teach you and we will come out exceedingly and abundantly better than we ever could ask or imagine.

3. Your infirmity is NOT your identity, but it can become my authority.

The enemy tries to use infirmities to lame us and maim us. Mephibosheth's name means "destroyer of shame." This is not going to become a "way of life," but instead a way to "more abundant life."

A friend of ours sent us some devotion cards that have Scriptures on them. When we are at the Shepherd's House, I usually read one each morning at breakfast. That particular morning right after listening to that message my devotion card was this:

> Don't fear, Rick! The Lord says, "I have redeemed you and called you by name. You're Mine! When you pass through the waters, you won't drown. When you walk through the fire, you won't be burned."
> (from Isaiah 43:1–2)

9 BIRTHING SOMETHING NEW

At the beginning of 2021, I had been praying for the Lord to give me a Scripture for our family. I was actually surprised as a very short time later I felt like He gave me Isaiah 43:18-19, "Do not remember the former things, Nor consider the things of old. Behold, I will do a new thing, Now it shall spring forth; Shall you not know it? I will even make a road in the wilderness And rivers in the desert."

"Do not remember the former things," the Scripture says, but what things? We're supposed to forget the things that have held us back, the things that, if they were removed from our life, would make it SO MUCH BETTER! Maybe it's a job condition, a health condition, your marriage, your children or someone in your family. Now, I know that we are not to deny reality, and I'm not saying that. But I do believe that Satan wants us to be so focused on the past and the way things have been for who knows how long that we can't move forward. Stop meditating and giving consideration to the FORMER THINGS....why? Because the Lord will do a new thing!

In verse 19, the word for "I will do" is the Hebrew word "asah" meaning refinement or creativity. A few words later in that same verse, He says, "I will make." The Hebrew word is "sum," meaning to place in a location, to appoint, to establish a new relationship, to assign something to someone, to bring about a change. It also means to set aside something for special purposes. Don't DWELL on the past but DECLARE God's Word over your future! I realize that this may sound like religious church-talk to some—a formula, if you will. But I'm talking about genuine, Spirit-led prayer and meditation on God's Word and then speaking it OUT LOUD OVER YOURSELF or YOUR SITUATION!

Years ago my parents had a beach house that they miraculously acquired in 1986. Located in the Florida panhandle, it was the perfect beach vacation home. Our whole family absolutely loved that place. Pam and I enjoyed it immensely over the years, and when our children came along, they loved it also. As time went by, my mom passed away and my dad lost interest in it completely. We hung on to it a few more years, but eventually the time came when it needed to be sold. Pam and I went down to clean it out when the time came, as it was being transferred to the new owner. All of the papers were signed, and it was time for us to leave our keys on the kitchen table and lock the door. We had raised our kids there, even brought their friends there. I could show you where the screws were still fastened under the deck where once a swing held our babies while my mom was inside preparing supper. That morning before we left, I had gone on a walk thinking about many memories of that wonderful family home. I felt the Lord speak to me that day, and here is what He impressed upon my heart: "I can't move you on to the future things that I have for you if you keep holding on to the things in the past." Later, Pam and I laid the keys on the table, held hands, and prayed. We then locked the door and walked out. And guess what? The Lord was absolutely true to His Word as the Shepherd's House was eventually birthed as a result of that decision! God is Good!

In the last chapter, I talked briefly about the number 40. Over the last few years, I've studied what certain numbers mean in the Bible. The number ten will always represent a test. It also represents "a setting in order." There were ten plagues in Egypt, Ten Commandments, David brought ten loaves and ten cheeses to the battle where he fought Goliath. The word "tithe" means ten percent. Of course it is a test of faith as we tithe ten percent and give this first. You will find this all through the Bible. However, the number 40 represents a time of sowing, a chronos time, if you will. Times of sowing are what bring about times of reaping or kairos times. If we don't know the difference spiritually, we will become discouraged and possibly give up when our blessing is right around the corner.

On July 7, 2020, the bronchoscopy was performed that confirmed adenocarcinoma in my lungs. If you count each week until the week of April 12th, you will count exactly 40 weeks. On April 15th of that week, I had my fourth CT scan. When I met with Dr. E. for my results, he told me that with the exception of some scarring, my scan looked like a NORMAL HEALTHY PERSON!

Here is the email to our victory prayer team right after that:

Hey Gang,

Just wanted to report MORE VICTORY to the Victory Team! I saw both of my doctors on Monday, (Dr. E.-radiologist & Dr. W.-oncologist). I had the CT scan this past Thursday & both doctors were texting about it on Friday. I saw Dr. E. first & he told me that the scan looked like a "normal healthy person with the exception of some scarring"! I am so grateful to the Lord for all that HE HAS DONE & IS DOING!!!

They want to continue the maintenance chemo so as to ensure that there is NOTHING LEFT!!! The plan is to have another PetScan in three months....so keep us in your prayers as we navigate the future. Also, Dr. W. expected my white count to have gone down & had planned for another Neulasta shot.... but guess what??? My count has actually gone up!!!!

I've been speaking a declaration of scripture over myself almost nightly & I had added to the declaration that "my white blood count increase & stay up"!!! Folks God's Word is POWERFUL!!!! Isaiah 55:10-11 says "For as the rain comes down, and the snow from heaven, And do not return there, But water the earth, And make it bring forth and bud, That it may give seed to the sower And bread to the eater, So shall My word be that goes forth from My mouth; It shall not return to Me void, But it shall accomplish what I please, And it shall prosper in the thing for which I sent it."

I encourage you to SPEAK GOD'S WORD OVER YOUR SITUATION!

The Lord has brought me SOOO far from where this all started. Many times I have reminded myself & thanked the Lord for:

* being able to eat freely without trouble of swallowing or choking.

* no longer wheezing when I breathe.

* and finally, NO MORE COUGHING!!!!

The Lord is OUR BEST FRIEND, OUR HEALER, OUR DELIVERER, OUR VICTORY!!! As Stone & Hayden's song says "My God is STRONG!"

Thank you for your prayers!!! We are so blessed to have friends like you! May God Richly pour out His manifold blessings & power upon YOU!!

We love you all,

Rick & Pam

In Numbers 13, there were 12 spies that were sent to spy out the promised land. Along with Joshua and Caleb, there were ten other leaders, heads of tribes that accompanied them. Notice these were not just randomly chosen men; these were men that were at the top of their tribes. Again, we see the number 40 as these men were 40 days investigating the condition of the land and the people to bring back a report as to how best to conquer this land. Upon returning, they reported their findings to Moses.

The report started out pretty good; "Truly it flows with milk and honey," they said. "And here is some of the fruit of the land." Then it went downhill from there. "Nevertheless, the people who dwell there are strong; the cities are fortified and very large; moreover we saw the descendants of Anak there." Then Caleb quieted the people and said, "Let us go up at once and take possession, for we are well able to overcome it."

Why were there such differing opinions among the same "group" of people? Hadn't they all seen the miraculous parting of the Red Sea, the mighty plagues that God sent against Pharaoh and the Egyptians? Why were there only two out of twelve (16.6%), of the top leaders that saw it differently? It sounds like 10 of them visited a different country than Joshua and Caleb. By the way, the number 12 represents "government." These 12 men—leaders, heads of tribes—should have been leading the way and setting the tone. Obviously, this was not the case.

You see, it all comes down to perspective. If you read on at the end of that chapter, they even say, "There we saw the giants and we were like grasshoppers in our OWN SIGHT, and SO WE WERE IN THEIR SIGHT," (emphasis mine). Did you catch that how they viewed themselves determined how others saw them? Isn't that so true? When we walk in confidence and faith, others see that and it's even contagious. Our spouses, our children, our friends—all perceive our outlook on life, our perspective. But how did Joshua and Caleb get to be like that? How or why did they possess such courage and confidence? Look at the next chapter in Numbers 14:24, "But my servant Caleb, because he has a different spirit in him and has followed Me fully, I will bring into the land where he went, and his descendants shall inherit it."

I believe that Caleb and Joshua had courageous hearts. They had faith that God was well able to perform what He had promised. This pleased God. Just like the Bible tells us, "But without faith it is impossible to please Him, for he who comes to God must believe that He is, and that He is a rewarder of those who diligently seek Him," (Hebrews 11:6). If we are to be faith-filled people we have to do what the Bible says: "So then faith comes by hearing, and hearing by the word of God," (Romans 10:17 NKJV).

The Bible tells us that "[We] will know them by their fruits" (good or bad). "Do men gather grapes from thornbushes or figs from thistles?" (Matthew 7:16 NKJV). The Bible goes on to say that the generation of those represented by the ten spies that brought back the evil report could not enter because of unbelief. I don't know about you, but I don't want to be around faithless or unbelieving people. I want to surround myself with Joshuas and Calebs!

I also believe that one of the tell-tale signs of negative people is complaining and murmuring. Is that not what describes the generation of Israelites that were not permitted to enter the promised land? Just like joy and enthusiasm are contagious attitudes, so is complaining and grumbling. Again, from the abundance of our hearts the mouth speaks. It really boils down to this simple phrase: "Show me your friends and I will show you your future."

I can only imagine my response to being diagnosed with stage four adenocarcinoma if I weren't a Christian. Of course it was a shock to all of us. I talked about that earlier in the book. However, after getting past the initial shock of what was happening to me, we had to choose how we would respond. I will never forget what my grandmother told me years ago. She told me, "Fear knocked, faith opened the door, and no one was there!" You might have to think about that one a little bit! When we respond to life's problems with faith, they cannot stand. The Bible tells us, "So Jesus answered and said to them, 'Assuredly, I say to you, if you have faith and do not doubt, you will not only do what was done to the fig tree, but also if you say to this mountain, 'Be removed and be cast into the sea,' it will be done. And whatever things you ask in prayer, believing, you will receive,'" (Matthew 21:21-22 NKJV).

So your spirit man—where we connect with God and hear His voice—as well as your soul (mind, will, and emotions), needs to be healthy. It's kind of like what Dr W. said to me when I first started the chemo treatments. He said, "We're going to throw a lot at this disease. If you're not healthy, you can't take it." So our mind, will, emotions, and spirit-man needs to be healthy, courageous, and full of faith. Of course the Lord will help us in these areas if we ask Him. I'm just saying that just like a weak-bodied person would struggle physically, a weak-minded or faithless person will struggle mentally and psychologically. And, as you might imagine, mentally and psychologically is where the spiritual battle for our well-being in all areas is fought.

On May 21, 2021, I wrote in my journal about a dove that laid two eggs in a flower pot on our back deck. This has never happened before after being in our house for almost 22 years! While thinking about it this morning, I thought the Holy Spirit—the presence of God—has built a nest at our house and brought new life! But not just new life....double! This actually happened twice in the same summer!

As most of you know, a dove represents the Spirit of God because of the story in Luke 3:22: "And the Holy Spirit descended in bodily form like a dove upon Him, and a voice came from heaven which said, 'You are My beloved Son; in You I am well pleased.'" Later, I read in the One Year Bible about the Lord giving Job twice as much as before: "And the LORD restored Job's losses when he prayed for his friends. Indeed the LORD gave Job twice as much as he had before," (Job 42:10 NKJV). A few verses later, the Bible has this to say about Job: "Now the LORD blessed the latter days of Job more than his beginning; for he had fourteen thousand sheep, six thousand camels, one thousand yoke of oxen, and one thousand female donkeys. He also had seven sons and three daughters. And he called the name of the first Jemimah, the name of the second Keziah, and the name of the third Keren-Happuch. In all the land were found no women so beautiful as the daughters of Job; and their father gave them an inheritance among their brothers. After this Job lived one hundred and forty years, and saw his children and grandchildren for four generations. So Job died, old and full of days," (Job 42:10, 12-17 NKJV).

I absolutely believe that the Lord is going to bless us like this—not because He owes us anything, but because He is good! One of the things that I've learned from being a parent is that there is nothing that gives me more joy than seeing my children blessed. I absolutely love to give to them and bless them! Pam and I will sometimes ask each other if we should give this or that because we can give too much—to their detriment. Therefore, we need the wisdom of the Holy Spirit to keep things in balance. But any good parent understands what I'm saying.

We were approaching one year into this battle when I wrote the following email to the Victory Prayer Team on June 1st:

Good afternoon Victory Team.

I am currently taking the sixth maintenance chemo treatment as I write this email. I have been praying daily over my white count & of course taking the Neulasta periodically. Today my count was 5.0 which may be the highest it's been....at least for awhile! I've actually started back traveling some the last month and it is so wonderful!

While walking and praying this morning I reminded the Lord that one year ago I was dying & didn't know it. But the Lord rescued me at the perfect moment! I know that I've repeated this many times, but four symptoms were getting worse. Sometimes choking when I would eat, wheezing when I breathed as one of my airways was virtually closed shut, coughing & coughing. One of the worst things was watching how my family reacted and how it affected them...it broke my heart!

The pangs of death surrounded me, And the floods of ungodliness made me afraid. The sorrows of Sheol surrounded me; The snares of death confronted me. In my distress I, (we) called upon the Lord, And cried out to my, God; He heard my voice from His temple, And my cry came before Him, even to His ears. Psalm 18:4-6

I reached out to you all to join us and lock shields together. Over the next eight months We all WATCHED GOD PERFORM HIS MIGHTY ACTS RIGHT BEFORE OUR EYES & DELIVER ME!

While I've probably taught hundreds of Sunday School lessons & led multiple small groups, (often speaking about the faithfulness of God), we should not think it strange to one day be attacked by the enemy to "just see if we really believe what we say we believe!" And while it isn't a pleasant path, we must remember the wine only comes from the crushed grapes; the most precious perfume only comes from the broken alabaster box. Just know this-God IS FAITHFUL!!!!!

We love you all!
Rick & Pam

10 VICTORY BELONGS TO JESUS

While I have already talked briefly about the number 7 meaning perfection and divine manifestation, I would like to talk more about it here. On July 7, 2020 (7/7/20), the bronchoscopy I had confirmed the adenocarcinoma in my lungs. Exactly one year later, July 7, 2021 (7/7/21—I'm not making this up), I had a PET scan that revealed that everything was gone except for scar tissue. Dr. E. asked us if we wanted to see the scan. We went back into his office, where he brought up my scan on his computer. There was nothing present except scar tissue where the tumor in my lower left lung looked like it had exploded! There were just fragments that Dr. E said was scar tissue. It was absolutely amazing to see what it looked like before and after!

Here is the email to our prayer team that followed this wonderful news:

Good afternoon Victory Team!

About one year ago this team was assembled as Pam and I were facing the battle for our lives (literally). I knew the Lord was speaking to me as I was reading the One Year Bible daily. Immediately following the diagnosis Pastor Larry Stockstill's devotion was about assembling a group of people that will commit to praying until the battle turns.

Well, you guys are that team and you have been so FAITHFUL to come alongside Pam and me! We are forever grateful for this!

Yesterday I got the results of a one year PET scan compared to the very first one. All I can say is WOW!!! Dr. E. took us back to his office where we actually got to view the pictures not just read the report. While all of the results are AMAZING, the one that stood out the most to me was the tumor where they believe this originated from, located in the left lower part of my lung. It was absolutely OBLITERATED!! It looked like it had exploded into nothing but fragments, which Dr. E. says is scar tissue.

Both Dr. E. and Dr. W. are very pleased with all of these great results. Dr. W. told me that I had done better than most and had done so from the very start. I know why that is and I give God ALL the glory!!!!!

The plan moving forward is to continue the maintenance chemo every three weeks for three months then scan again, (Dr. W. has a plan and he sticks with the plan...especially if it's working ☺). I told him that he was my doctor and I will do what he says. At the end of the day, it's all about what the Lord's will is as to how we continue. I absolutely believe and am convinced, that He has healed me as the results speak for themselves. However, I've never tried to dictate "how" He would heal other than speak & believe His Word....He's the potter, I'm the clay.

He has taught me many things over this year and I feel like I've grown spiritually. I know this would NOT have happened any other way. And, while I don't believe the Lord was behind this, He certainly has used it!

I will keep you posted on future events. For now just continue to pray for the treatments to accomplish what they are meant to do, no adverse side effects, and the Doctors to be led of the Lord.

We love you all!

Rick & Pam

In addition to studying the meaning of the number 7, I have also spent some time researching the letters of the Hebrew alphabet. Most of what the next two paragraphs contain was taken from the livingword.org.au website. Unlike our English alphabet, the Hebrew alphabet has 22 letters. The seventh letter of the Hebrew is zayin.

ז

As you can see, it looks like a scepter, the symbol of authority of a king. In the New Testament, there are seven declarations of Jesus as King. The last one is found in Revelation 19:16, "And He has on His robe and on His thigh a name written: KING OF KINGS AND LORD OF LORDS." In Genesis 1, we see the phrase "and God said" many times. The numeric value of that phrase is 343 or 7 X 7 X 7. We know from John 1:1 that "in the beginning was the Word, and the Word was with God and the Word was God." When we hear and read the words "and God said" in Genesis 1, and then we know from John 1:1 that Jesus is the Word of God, we can start to see the picture. God's Word, the Bible, is Jesus! The Bible says that every knee shall bow and every tongue confess that Jesus is Lord! In the same way, EVERYTHING MUST BOW TO GOD'S WORD! So, now do you see why it is so important to speak God's Word over every situation, sin, and sickness that we face? It has to BOW! The meaning of "bow" is yield or submit. NOTHING can stand against God! No wonder the Bible declares, "Greater is He Who is in you than he that is in the world," in I John 4:4, and "What then shall we say to these things? If God is for us, who can be against us? Yet, in all these things we are more than conquerors through Him who loved us," (Romans 8:31, 37 NKJV). I'm sure I could keep going but you get the point. The bottom line is this: there is NOTHING TOO HARD FOR GOD!

Allow me to continue. As I stated in the paragraph above, the Bible says, "Therefore God also has highly exalted Him and given Him the name which is above every name, that at the name of Jesus every knee should bow, of those in heaven, and of those on earth, and of those under the earth, and that every tongue should confess that Jesus Christ is Lord, to the glory of God the Father," (Philippians 2:9-11). The Greek word for name is "onoma," and it means the attribute, character, and authority of the person. Think about when you hear someone's name. What goes through your mind? Immediately upon hearing their name, you have some sort of association with that name. When we think of Jesus and say His Name, all of His attributes, character, ALL AUTHORITY is associated with His Name—healing, salvation, deliverance, peace, and provision. Please don't miss this, it is as though Jesus Himself is standing here interceding in our situation! And that's because HE IS! How powerful is that?

Our church launches small groups three times a year. In addition to teaching Sunday school for many years, I have also led many small groups. While just about all of our groups have been some type of Bible study, Pam and I have hosted a wide variety of groups. Most of the time I use someone else's material, but occasionally I write my own, especially if I believe strongly that it is what's needed.

As the Fall Small Group Semester approached, I knew in my heart the Lord was stirring up all of the things that He had been showing me in the last year. We decided to lead a group that we called "What to Do When You Don't Know What to Do!" I took the title from the Bible story in II Chronicles 20:

"It happened after this that the people of Moab with the people of Ammon, and others with them besides the Ammonites, came to battle against Jehoshaphat. Then some came and told Jehoshaphat, saying, "A great multitude is coming against you from beyond the sea, from Syria; and they are in Hazazon Tamar" (which is En Gedi). And Jehoshaphat feared, and set himself to seek the LORD, and proclaimed a fast throughout all Judah. So Judah gathered together to ask help from the LORD; and from all the cities of Judah they came to seek the LORD. Then Jehoshaphat stood in the assembly of Judah and Jerusalem, in the house of the LORD, before the new court, and said: "O LORD God of our fathers, are You not God in heaven, and do You not rule over all the kingdoms of the nations, and in Your hand is there not power and might, so that no one is able to withstand You? Are You not our God, who drove out the inhabitants of this land before Your people Israel, and gave it to the descendants of Abraham Your friend forever? And they dwell in it, and have built You a sanctuary in it for Your name, saying, 'If disaster comes upon us—sword, judgment, pestilence, or famine—we will stand before this temple and in Your presence (for Your name is in this temple), and cry out to You in our affliction, and You will hear and save.' And now, here are the people of Ammon, Moab, and Mount Seir—whom You would not let Israel invade when they came out of the land of Egypt, but they turned from them and did not destroy them— here they are, rewarding us by coming to throw us out of Your possession which You have given us to inherit. O our God, will You not judge them? For we have no power against this great multitude that is coming against us; nor do we know what to do, but our eyes are upon You," (II Chronicles 20:1-12 NKJV).

There were eight things that I felt like the Lord had taught us specifically that I wanted to incorporate into the small group. My email to our Victory Prayer Team lists those topics:

Victory Team....

Hey Gang! I hope everyone is doing wonderful as we approach this beautiful Fall season! I just want to report back to all of you what is going on with Pam & me. I am doing great & continuing the maintenance chemo treatments every three weeks. I'm back to traveling more on my job & testifying to those the Lord puts on my heart about the great healing work that He has performed in my life. It's still so awesome what the Lord has done for me! I'm FOREVER GRATEFUL TO HIM!!!

So, a few weeks ago I believe the Lord put it in my heart to lead a small group for the Fall Semester that we're calling "What to do when you don't know what to do." Obviously, you know where this title came from. The main theme is from II Chron. 20:1-20 where the vast army came against Jehoshaphat and this is what Jehoshaphat says in verse 12; "O our God, will You not judge them? For we have no power against this great multitude that is coming against us; nor do we know what to do, but our eyes are upon You."

These are key lessons the Lord taught me this last year that I have converted into Small Group Weekly Topics:

The importance of knowing Jesus & giving yourself totally to Him & putting Him first.

Look at Jesus & how to stay focused on Him; Peter walking on the water & Worship!

Our part & God's part-Health, diet, rest, & exercise.

God's Word-know what it says!!! Declaring & Decreeing His Word!

Our Thoughts & Our Words.

Disarming the enemy.

Prayer-Victory Team/Pam praying@4am

The power of Communion & The Holy Spirit.

YOU played a huge role in all of this as you continued to faithfully lift us up in prayer. ONLY by the power of GOD am I here now writing this email as I was dying. But today, I have never been more ALIVE!

Thank you all for what you do for the LORD & praying for us! I just wanted to let you know how the Lord is using what happened for His Glory!

We love you all,

Rick & Pam

Wow, what a wonderful small group it was! I absolutely loved every minute of it! We concluded the group at the Shepherd's House for a Saturday afternoon of just food, fun, and fellowship! It was awesome!

By the way, if you're wondering how the story ended in II Chronicles, here it is:

"And when he, (King Jehoshaphat), had consulted with the people, he appointed those who should sing to the LORD, and who should praise the beauty of holiness, as they went out before the army and were saying: "Praise the LORD, For His mercy endures forever. Now when they began to sing and to praise, the LORD set ambushes against the people of Ammon, Moab, and Mount Seir, who had come against Judah; and they were defeated. For the people of Ammon and Moab stood up against the inhabitants of Mount Seir to utterly kill and destroy them. And when they had made an end of the inhabitants of Seir, they helped to destroy one another. So when Judah came to a place overlooking the wilderness, they looked toward the multitude; and there were their dead bodies, fallen on the earth. No one had escaped," (II Chronicles 20:21-24 NKJV).

Now we have talked about about worship, but not about praise. Praise is an offensive weapon! I absolutely believe that when we gather in our church on Sunday morning and we begin to join corporately with the congregation and sing praise to the Lord, something supernatural happens. I personally believe that the Lord dispatches angels to move into the week ahead and fight spiritual battles that we will face. When we actively participate in praising our God, He goes before us and fights our battles just like He did for Jehoshaphat and the people of Judah. By the way, do you know what the name Judah means? "Praise!"

Finally, as I conclude this chapter, allow me to talk about the number ten. I've come to learn that the number ten means "test." I learned much of this through reading Pastor Robert Morris' book, *The Blessed Life*. However, I've seen this play out in my own life as well. You see, the the number ten is found in the word "tithe." Tithing means "a tenth," or ten percent of our income. I've spent most of my life as a Christian. I was saved when I was 15 years old. Early on, I was taught about tithing. Even though I didn't fully understand what it was all about, I have practiced tithing most of my life. One of my first jobs involved greasing a man's eighteen wheeler coal truck. There were grease fittings all over that thing! I would ride my motorcycle over to his shop, put on a pair of coveralls, fill up the grease gun, and start to work. It was a dirty job! More than once I would be all contorted up under the rear axle of that thing when the grease gun would run out of grease! I would have to crawl out, fill the gun back up with grease, and start again. I was paid $5.00 each time I would grease the truck and trailer. Obviously, that was along time ago. But here's the point that I want to make: on Sunday morning, I would put .50 (ten percent), into a tithing envelope and pay my tithes. You see, tithing is a test. It's a test of putting things in order. Our finances will never be in order if we don't tithe.

But tithing really isn't about the money; it's about our hearts and putting God first. There are powerful blessings, favor, and benefit to tithing also. In the book of Malachi, we read, "'Bring all the tithes into the storehouse, That there may be food in My house, And try Me now in this,' Says the LORD of hosts, 'If I will not open for you the windows of heaven And pour out for you such blessing that there will not be room enough to receive it. And I will rebuke the devourer for your sakes, So that he will not destroy the fruit of your ground, Nor shall the vine fail to bear fruit for you in the field,' Says the LORD of hosts; 'And all nations will call you blessed, For you will be a delightful land,' Says the LORD of hosts," (Malachi 3:10-12 NKJV).

You see, tithing is a test because it takes faith to pay our tithes first before we pay our bills, our mortgage, or spend it on what we might want to buy. Some people will do all of the above and then give to the Lord out of what is left over. You will find the principle of tithing all through the Bible. Consider this story in I Kings 17 during a severe famine: "Then the word of the LORD came to him, (Elijah), saying, 'Arise, go to Zarephath, which belongs to Sidon, and dwell there. See, I have commanded a widow there to provide for you.' So he arose and went to Zarephath. And when he came to the gate of the city, indeed a widow was there gathering sticks. And he called to her and said, 'Please bring me a little water in a cup, that I may drink.' And as she was going to get it, he called to her and said, 'Please bring me a morsel of bread in your hand.' So she said, 'As the LORD your God lives, I do not have bread, only a handful of flour in a bin, and a little oil in a jar; and see, I am gathering a couple of sticks that I may go in and prepare it for myself and my son, that we may eat it, and die.' And Elijah said to her, 'Do not fear; go and do as you have said, but make me a small cake from it first, and bring it to me; and afterward make some for yourself and your son. For thus says the LORD God of Israel: 'The bin of flour shall not be used up, nor shall the jar of oil run dry, until the day the LORD sends rain on the earth.' So she went away and did according to the word of Elijah; and she and he and her household ate for many days. The bin of flour was not used up, nor did the jar of oil run dry, according to the word of the LORD which He spoke by Elijah," (I Kings 17:8-16 NKJV).

Fast forward several years later; I'm now married with a family of my own. Pam saw Pastor Robert on the television show "Life Today" with James and Betty Robison. Pastor Robert was talking about a book he had just written called *The Blessed Life*. As Pam heard Pastor Robert talk about this book, she somehow sensed in her heart that it was something that I needed to read, so she ordered it.

A few days later, the book arrived and she told me the story of how that she had come to order it. I began to read the book. It was one of those books that I could hardly put down. Even though I had tithed for most of my life, the Holy Spirit spoke to me so much as I read those pages! I had never heard anyone explain tithing and giving like Pastor Robert. He also said something that I will never forget. He said that Jesus was God's tithes! God gave His precious, only Son first—before anyone had ever given their heart to the Lord. The Bible says it like this: "But God demonstrates His own love toward us, in that while we were still sinners, Christ died for us," (Romans 5:8 NKJV).

I will never forget as I read that book how the Lord spoke to me. To be very transparent, I had paid our tithes but not on the money set aside for retirement. My reasoning was that this money will grow and compound with interest; one day, when I retire and start drawing it out, we'll tithe on it. I really think deep down, it was just an excuse. Pastor Robert talked about this specifically in the book. He asked the question, "Wouldn't you want your 401k to be blessed?" Well, this spoke to me, and while I knew that the Lord wasn't forcing me to do anything, nor did I feel condemned, I just knew in my heart it was a test! You see, we had built up a fair sum of money by now and to tithe on our 401k required coming up with a fairly large sum of money—at least to me! However, I sensed this was a pivotal moment in my life regarding obedience and trust in the Lord. So here's what I said to the Lord: "If You will help me, I will pay this sum of money. I don't know how yet, but I will do it."

Now, let me just clarify something here. I don't believe in giving to get. That's one of the topics that *The Blessed Life* covers clearly. God is not a slot machine where we insert our dollars and pull the lever looking to hit the jackpot! No, it's about our heart. Again, the Bible says it like this: "For where your treasure is, there your heart will be also," (Matthew 6:21 NKJV). God is after our hearts, because He knows that if He has our hearts, then He has us!

I received a promotion at work to the position of plant manager. I had served in the role of Superintendent at our facility for a few years, and the previous manager was retiring. They asked me if I wanted to be considered for this position, and I said yes. Along with this position came a company car. I owned a late model truck that I really liked, but no longer needed. I sold the truck, took the profit, and gave it to my church—in keeping with my statement to the Lord that if He would help me, I would tithe on my 401k. Again, I'm not trying to put my convictions on anyone else; I just know that this is what the Lord impressed upon me to do. The amount from the truck sale was only about one third of the total amount. In the meantime, another 401k account that I had with a previous company had been frozen when the division that I worked in was sold to another company. I can't remember all of the details, but right around this time the account was "unfrozen" and the funds released. When this happened, I rolled it over into another investment firm and took a distribution to finish paying the tithing amount.

I had never given that much money at one time in my whole life! It was exciting, and I never ever felt any regret as I knew that I was obeying what the Lord had put in my heart to do! I didn't expect anything in return; regardless, I knew the Lord would bless us for following Him in obedience.

A few months rolled by as I settled into my new role as plant manager when I received an email from our company car fleet manager. The email read something like, "It's time for you to go pick out your company vehicle." If I remember correctly, I dismissed the email received thinking to myself, *I already have a company vehicle.* A day or so later, another email came, explaining that my vehicle was a few years old; it was time to turn mine in for a new one. Not only that, for the first time in history, our company was offering a brand new, extended-cab Silverado as one of the choices! I could hardly believe what I was reading. Not barely six months earlier I had sold my truck and gave the profit to the church, and now I was to go down to the local Chevrolet dealership and pick out the color I wanted in a new truck.

Allow me to tell just one more short story about tithing. Back in chapter two, I described how my son, Stone, was telling us how he had been asking the Lord to challenge his faith. Well, what I didn't explain is that Stone told us something else that day that touched my heart so deeply. For some time, Pam and I had paid our tithes on our gross income. For many years, we had given ten percent based on our "net" income, or "after-tax income." In retrospect, it sounds ridiculous to even grapple over one versus the other. And I'm certainly not pushing my convictions on you. We just made the decision one day that if we really believed in the principle of giving, we didn't have to worry about what little difference that would make; we just decided to give right off the top every month. Well, I will never forget that day while Stone was talking about his faith being challenged; he also said that he had been thinking about his giving. He had made the decision to give based on his net income much like Pam and I did for many years. He went on to say that he had been asking the Lord to give His best and to heal me, but he wasn't giving his best. He said that day he made up his mind that he was going to give based on his gross pay. Now that may not seem like a big deal, but it is always a big deal when it comes to obedience and giving money. Again, it's not about works to earn God's blessings, but it's about our heart. God wants our hearts because He knows that if He has our hearts, He has us!

Can I ask you a question? Does the Lord have your heart? I'm not talking about money or giving, but about a genuine salvation experience with Him. I purposely inserted this paragraph in the book as I believe that, as you have been reading these pages, the Lord has been speaking to you. You may have tried to shake it off or even thought, "I'm a good person." I'm sure you are a good person. But it's not about being good. It's about a relationship with a Savior who loves you more than you can ever imagine. Maybe you've purchased this book because you've been diagnosed with a terrible disease like I was. Or maybe you just wanted to read this book. I don't know your circumstances. But I know someone that does. He knows everything about you. Better yet, He has come that we might have LIFE and have it more abundantly (John 10:10). Accepting Christ as Lord is really more about acknowledging Him when He knocks on your heart. Open the door; let Him come in. Simply say this and mean it from your heart: "Lord, I desire a relationship with You; I need You. I open my heart, my life for You to be Lord of it all. I'm sorry for my sins…I ask for Your forgiveness now and accept You as my Savior. In Your Name I pray, Amen."

That's awesome! I'm so proud of you and your decision to accept Christ! If you made that decision and would like some help in your next steps, please send an email to pmcree17@gmail.com.

11 BE PATIENT

On October 22, 2021, I had a follow up CT scan. The following Monday, I saw Dr. W for a maintenance treatment. As I have stated earlier in the book, Dr. W doesn't show much excitement, nor does he come across as very optimistic. However, on this visit, he said something that I had never heard him say before. Dr. W said, "I believe the cancer is gone!" Now, we had been believing that for many months, but to hear him say it was miraculous! I got sort of choked up and told both Dr. W and his physician assistant that I knew that they had never sat where I was sitting before. And while I am so grateful for their care and help, I wanted to let them know that people like me just needed some hope. However, I thanked them for their kindness and care as I knew the Lord had used them in the healing process.

A few weeks later, in mid-November, I was out on the deck on a Wednesday morning. I was reminiscing about what I had gone through back in July 2020. I was reading what I had written in my journal that day, dated July 7, 2020: "Death wrapped its ropes around me; the terrors of the grave overtook me. I saw only trouble and sorrow. Then I called on the name of the Lord: 'Please, Lord, save me!' How kind the Lord is! How good he is! So merciful, this God of ours! The Lord protects those of childlike faith; I was facing death, and he saved me. Let my soul be at rest again, for the Lord has been good to me. He has saved me from death, my eyes from tears, my feet from stumbling. And so I walk in the Lord's presence as I live here on earth!" (Psalm 116:3-9 NLT).

As I read those verses, I thought, what wonderful words—this would be something great to read at Thanksgiving this year! I felt compelled to read the One Year Bible for that day and the devotional from Pastor Larry Stockstill. Here is what it said:

Are you going through a severe trial today? If so, your mind must settle certain issues. First, your reaction to the trial should be one of joy, for the testing of your faith develops perseverance (James 1:2-3). Rejoice when trials come your way, because without a test there can be no testimony. Second, you should remember that if you persevere and withstand the test, you will receive the crown of life (v12). All your earthly difficulties are simply adding jewels to your eternal crown and rewards. That is a life-changing way to look at trials now isn't it? Finally, you should never blame God for all of your trials. He does not tempt you to sin and only gives you what is good. Whatever is good and perfect comes to us from God above, who created all heaven's lights, (v17). Always remember "how kind the Lord is! How good He is! So merciful, this God of ours! Psalm 116:5 The summary of the matter-trials are working in your character, they are temporary, and God is concerned about your trials. One day you will be on the other side of the trial, saying to yourself as the Psalmist said, "Now I can rest again, for the Lord has been so good to me," (Psalm 116:7).

Nobody but the Lord could have orchestrated what happened that day! There are 365 daily devotions in the year and I just happened to have read in my journal the very same one for that day! You're not going to get me to believe this was just coincidence! God is good and always knows what we need and when we need it! Ever since that day, there has been another level of peace that "stands guard over my heart and mind" as Philippians 4:7 says.

One of the things I've come to realize is that we don't wait well. We live in an instant society where practically everything is immediate! I have to admit, waiting can be challenging for me as well. But waiting reveals something about us. Daniel fasted for 21 days before the angel of the Lord came. Jesus prayed and fasted for 40 days before His trial ended in the wilderness. Caleb waited 45 years before he was able to lay claim to the mountain that he was promised! When the first CT scan revealed about fifty percent of the cancer had been destroyed, I was disappointed. Why? Because we don't wait well; we want it over with NOW! But God doesn't work according to our timetable. Eventually, I would have to learn that if I was going to fully trust the Lord, I would have to learn to trust His timetable as well. Remember—during the crucifixion and the resurrection, there was a day between the two. Our pastor says it like this: "Saturday was the day between the pain and the promise." The Bible says it like this: "Therefore do not cast away your confidence, which has great reward. For you have need of endurance, so that after you have done the will of God, you may receive the promise," (Hebrews 10:35-36 NKJV).

When the Israelites saw that Moses had delayed his returning from receiving the Ten Commandments, they turned aside and made themselves another god that they proclaimed had saved them. The waiting got the best of them. Their faith was shallow even though they had witnessed the mighty acts of God— ten plagues poured out on the Egyptians while they were kept perfectly safe! However, it takes faith and patience to wait. Waiting reveals WHO YOU REALLY ARE. If we don't guard our hearts and minds, we will give in to the thoughts of the enemy. We'll think, "God has forsaken you," or, "Why are you waiting?" "You need to take matters into your own hands." Then, the ultimate goal of the enemy of our soul is to get us to erect a stronghold, (the golden calf), and get us to bow to that idol, convincing us that "other means" are what we need to resort to. He says, "As for this God you serve, He has abandoned you!"

In January of 2022, I completed 45 years of working on my job. I know that many may find this hard to believe, but I went to work at 18 after graduating from high school. I went to work for Gerber Baby Food in a coil, coating, and lithography plant. Later we were bought out by General Foods, Maxwell House Coffee Division, and finally purchased by a large food can company where I currently continue to be employed. I have never had to look for another job. Today I have the greatest job ever and appreciate it immensely.

But it hasn't always been that way. You see, there were times when I was under much stress, even agonizing at times about the way things were. At one point, the plant where I had worked for 31 years closed. It was like losing a large family of friends I had known most of my life. I will never forget that at that time, Pam and I had our two young children still at home and didn't know what or where our future would lead. We decided to fast and pray for the entire week. A few of the days I would come home at lunch and go up to my office and pray. On one particular occasion, I remember coming down after prayer and sitting next to Pam on the couch. I remember saying these words to her: "I don't know what the Lord has for us, but it will be more than we can imagine." Not long after that, my company asked me to move into an engineering position that allowed me to work from home. We didn't have to relocate and it has turned out to be the greatest job that I have ever known! I absolutely love my job and the people!

I'm convinced that somewhere along the line in our iPhone, iPad, Apple Watch era, (by the way, I happen to own all three of these items), we have become so distracted and impatient that we miss—not only the opportunities in front of us, but in our impatience, we can't wait for things to move into place as the Lord desires to orchestrate our lives. Life isn't just about getting from point "A" to point "B" as fast as you can. It's about the journey itself and being PREPARED for the journey and what's ahead!

"Have you not known? Have you not heard? The everlasting God, the LORD, The Creator of the ends of the earth, Neither faints nor is weary. His understanding is unsearchable. He gives power to the weak, And to those who have no might He increases strength. Even the youths shall faint and be weary, And the young men shall utterly fall, But those who wait on the LORD Shall renew their strength; They shall mount up with wings like eagles, They shall run and not be weary, They shall walk and not faint," (Isaiah 40:28-31 NKJV).

12 FAITH IN ACTION

A few weeks ago, at the time of this writing, my sweet Aunt passed away unexpectedly. She was my dad's last living sibling. I was traveling and on my way to the airport when I received the news. I was shocked. The last time I saw my aunt was at the funeral of my dad's last living brother.

She was a godly woman, full of faith and the Spirit of God. I loved her so much! We used to sit around during the holidays when family would visit and no one was in a hurry and talk about the goodness of the Lord and the marvelous acts He's performed in all of our lives. I will never forget those times—or her. When I saw her at my uncle's funeral just over a year before, the first thing she said to me was: "The Lord's going to heal you!" Before we left the cemetery that day, I asked her to lay her hands on me and pray for me. Boy, could that woman pray! And, you knew that you had been prayed for when she was done!

The reason I bring up that story is this: I had planned to have our extended family come up to the Shepherd's House for a family gathering. But more than that, I wanted my son and daughter, along with their spouses, to experience the rich Christian heritage that my grandmother Tezzie had passed down through her faithful life and prayers. My granddad had accepted the Lord late in his life and been transformed by God. I'm sure my grandmother played a huge role in that! But here is the point that I want to make: I failed to act and plan this event that I had dreamed about until it was too late. I had good intentions, but good intentions don't get the job done.

At the end of the last chapter, I talked about being patient. At the expense of contradicting myself, I'm now going to talk about action! The Bible tells us, "There is a time for all things," (Ecclesiastes 3:1). In this case, I would say—a time to wait and a time to act. The problem comes in when we don't know which one to do. When the Lord puts something in our heart—an idea, or dream—we need to act on it, even if it is only start to pray about it, plan, and count the cost. I don't think the Lord puts things in our heart to make us think, "Yeah, one day that would be awesome to do, Lord!' We think things will always be as they are now. But deep down, we know better. God, awaken our hearts to seize the moments and use the resources You have given us to make a difference NOW! What will we do *different* between now and next Christmas? Will we just let another year go by without having goals or vision for something new?

The book of James said that we are to be doers of the Word, not just hearers only! "But be doers of the word, and not hearers only, deceiving yourselves. For if anyone is a hearer of the word and not a doer, he is like a man observing his natural face in a mirror; for he observes himself, goes away, and immediately forgets what kind of man he was. But he who looks into the perfect law of liberty and continues in it, and is not a forgetful hearer but a doer of the work, this one will be blessed in what he does," (James 1:22-25 NKJV).

One chapter over, James has this to say: "What does it profit, my brethren, if someone says he has faith but does not have works? Can faith save him? If a brother or sister is naked and destitute of daily food, and one of you says to them, "Depart in peace, be warmed and filled," but you do not give them the things which are needed for the body, what does it profit? Thus also faith by itself, if it does not have works, is dead," (James 2:14-17

NKJV). I feel like my life has been saved. As I said earlier in the book, I was literally dying and the Lord saved me! I can't spend the remaining part of my life just drifting here and there. No! I must live with purpose everyday and seize every moment. I must use every resource and leverage it for the Kingdom of God. Our lives aren't meant to be saved but given away.

When Pam and I decided to build the Shepherd's House, the enemy fought me on it. My dad had always taught me to save my money. He was brought up during the Depression. He was born in 1924 and was raised during some very hard times. He worked his way out of poverty by educating himself, working hard, and saving his money. Dad passed on his financial advice to me, and it has greatly benefited us. To make a decision to invest heavily in this family lake house was a huge step for me. I can remember lying in bed at night with thoughts running through my head like, "What do you think you're doing?" "What makes you think you can afford a house like you're building?" Now, don't misunderstand; I'm not saying go out and spend money that you don't have on things that you don't need! Building this lake house was a carefully, calculated endeavor that had been given much thought. But there were several reasons that I needed to act when I did. I was 60 years old, the economy was great, and if I had waited, I would have been diagnosed with stage four lung cancer that would have stopped the process completely. Chances are the Shepherd's House would have never been a reality after that. I looked at the lake house as an investment in ETERNAL things, people, family, friends, and even folks we don't know.

A year or so ago my son invited a few guys that he worked with to come to the Shepherd's House for the weekend. Upon arrival, they came in and were totally taken back by the views of the lake and the wonderful home the Lord has blessed us with. They couldn't believe this was the place my son had invited them to. One of the guys went upstairs to put his things away and as he came out of his room, he said to Stone, "I don't know what it is about this place but I feel peace here." Stone pointed to the large sign above the fireplace that reads "The Shepherd's House" with Psalm 23 inscribed below. Stone said, "This is the Shepherd's House; my parents pray over this house. That's why you feel like you do."

Being decisive is important. The fact is, that when we waver or hesitate, doubt and even fear can try to influence us. There is never going to be the "perfect" time to act on things. If we're waiting for that time, it will never come. Quite often I've found that the Lord will not show us the next step until we have taken the first step. I remember reading something that Rick Warren said in his book *The Purpose Driven Life:* "Obedience unlocks understanding."

As I was nearing the two year mark of being on maintenance chemo, my doctor let me know that there would be some decisions to make. The choices were: stay on the same kind of treatment plan, stop the plan altogether, or begin a hybrid plan. Dr. W let me know that some people struggle with the decision because the medicine has become their security blanket. Pam and I began to pray about it, even though it wasn't time for the decision yet. One night, not too many days later, I wasn't even thinking about this, but just as I was about to get into bed, the Lord impressed upon me that He was going to speak to me about what to do regarding the treatment decision. He let me know that it would come through my devotion time with Him. I have to admit, the Lord is usually not that direct or plain with me. It was unusual for that to happen like it did.

The next morning as I was going out on the deck for my devotion time, I remembered what the Lord had impressed upon me the night before. When I read the One Year Bible, this was the devotion for that particular day: "Our lives are confused and insecure when we leave our Rock in order to build our lives on shifting sand. The rich fool thought he was secure in his barns and possessions, but he found out that his life was built on a false foundation."

I went on to read the Scripture for that day's Bible reading, and here is what it said: "Be strong and of good courage, fear not, nor be afraid of them; for the Lord thy God, He it is that goes with thee; He will not fail thee nor forsake thee," (Deuteronomy 31:6). Afterwards, in the New Testament I read Luke 12:25-32 about how God cares for the ravens and the lilies; how much more will He clothe us. It was obvious what the Lord was saying to me. The medicine can become something one depends on rather than God. It was exactly what Dr. W was telling me about regarding the "security blanket." God has certainly used the doctors and the medicine, and I'm not against it at all. However, the chemo drugs are very strong with very harmful toxins that one should carefully consider before taking for years! Once again, the Lord's faithful guidance showed us the next move, and we did so with tremendous confidence rather than fear.

As I said before, I have a greater appreciation for life today than ever before. I can remember early on in my treatment when we didn't have any evidence of how things were going other than our faith in the Lord and His Word. On one particular beautiful fall day, we were working along the shoreline of our lake property at the Shepherd's House. As I was working away, I remember looking up at Pam and thinking, *I bet she is thinking, "I don't want our life together to ever end."* Somehow, I felt like she was taking it all in, squeezing every drop out of days like that! It's sad to say, but for most, the reality is that we never fully value this life we have until it is threatened or gone. Why do we wait until funerals to say what should have been said while the person was alive? Hundreds of dollars are spent on flowers and plants, only to fade and die at the graveside of our friend or loved one. Life is precious and fleeting. Make it meaningful. Make it count! Do it now!

Back in chapter ten when I was describing tests that we go through, I mentioned the widow at Zarephath in I Kings 17. The word "Zarephat" comes from the word tsaraph which is the Hebrew word for "smelting place." Smelting is a process whereby ore is placed in a blast furnace and the heat is turned up until the impurities and gases are eliminated. You know, sometimes we're just full of gas and hot air! What the widow did not know is that she was in the smelting place about to be tested. If you recall, the famine had wiped out everyone's food resources, and she was on her way to make her last meal to eat and die. When the prophet Elijah asked her to make him a little cake first, the widow had a choice to make. Would she obey the man of God and act in faith, or would she respond in the flesh by looking only at the present circumstances?

In the New Testament, the Greek word equivalent to "tsaraph" is "dokimazo." It is found in James 1:3, which describes the "trying of your faith." Life's tests are designed by God to prepare, equip, and condition us for what is ahead. If we act in faith and pass the test, we move on. If we fail the test, then we can rest assured that it will come again in another form. However, it will be the same test. The unfortunate reality is that most folks go through life oblivious to these tests. Unable to recognize them as opportunities for growth and character development, we often respond with complaints and grumbling rather than seeing them for what they are.

To simplify this principle, it is kind of like training your child that the stove is hot. "No!" we say, "Don't touch that pot or that pan. That will burn you!" we say. But guess what? One day they touch it. I bet you never have to tell them again! Experience is different from explanation. Pain has a purpose, and while I do not believe that God causes all pain, He does use it to develop us.

13 CONCLUSION AND FINAL THOUGHTS

On New Year's Eve night leading into 2017, I had a dream that was so vivid and real. I normally don't pay any attention to my dreams, but this one was different. When I awakened that day, I wrote it down as I sensed that it meant something—I just didn't know what at the time. In my dream, I was in a classroom and an instructor was giving a test. It was some kind of science test. At first glance, the test was written in small print and hard to read. The test was to take 2.5 hours or so. I remember knowing that I was not prepared to take the test! It was one of those feelings like you may have experienced in school; you were given a major test, and, as soon as the test was handed to you, you realized that you didn't know the answer to any of the questions. One of the questions on the test was, "What is the season from December to May?" It had to do with the sun going down earlier. I remember thinking, "Is the answer winter? Or is it the solstice?" It was an open-book test. Upon studying my book, I found the answer was "harvest knowledge."

For a few years, I never knew what this dream meant. However, I believed from the beginning that it was significant. Since that time, I've come to believe that the dream means the following:

- I was in a classroom and an instructor was giving a test. It was some kind of science test. This represented the attack of sickness from Satan to take my life.

- At first glance, the test was written in small print and hard to read. The doctors had a very hard time identifying the cancer as the X-rays and prior diagnosis were incorrect, (acid reflux, allergies and asthma).

- The test was to take 2.5 hours or so. After the remaining maintenance treatments, it has encompassed 2.5 years.

- I was not prepared to take the test. It was one of those feelings like you may have experienced in school; you were given a major test, and, as soon as the test was handed to you, you realized that you didn't know the answer to any of the questions. While I believe that I was spiritually prepared for the test (only by the grace of God), it came out of nowhere and took me totally by surprise.

- It was an open-book test. The Word of God is our manual for life that I have studied often throughout the years. Early on, right after the diagnosis, I remember the feeling impressed by the Lord that studying God's Word was how I was going to get through this test and be victorious.

- One of the questions on the test was, "What is the season from December to May?" It had to do with the sun going down earlier. It was an open-book test. Upon studying my book, I found the answer was "harvest knowledge." I believe that this means the main purpose of the test that I encountered was to teach me:
  - The time is short.
  - Make everyday count.
  - At the end of the day, there is nothing more important than sharing our faith by being a witness to the lost (or harvest knowledge). Remember, we don't have to know all of the answers people ask,

nor can we save anybody. But we are simply to witness or tell from our perspective what the Lord has done in OUR lives.

Back in chapter six I mentioned a prophecy that was spoken over me when I was in my forties. As I said in chapter six, all these years I wasn't really sure what the prophecy meant, but I do believe this trial we faced plays a part in the fulfillment of it. What I'm about to tell you may be the strangest thing yet, but it's too amazing to not share. Do you remember earlier in the book I talked some about numbers and what they mean? I mentioned that one year to the exact date from the diagnosis (7/7/20-7/721), I had a PET scan that showed that all was clear. As you may remember, I told the nurse about the significance of the number seven. Well, when she went back to retrieve the radioactive tracer she said, "Well, there's that number again, 17.7!" That was the number on the tracer. I really didn't think too much about it, but later as I emerged from taking the scan, the first number that I saw on the PET scan display was 717. Again, I didn't give any of this much thought other than that the number seven kept popping up. However, I did write all of these numbers in my journal.

Fast forward to about nine months later. I was watching Kenneth Copeland and Professor Greg Stephens on a program talking about how the first five books of the Bible, referred to as the Pentateuch, are sometimes prophetic in corresponding to numbers. In other words, sometimes people will take the year such as 2020 and count from Genesis two thousand and twenty verses to see what scripture it is and if there is significance regarding what happened in that year.

To be honest, I had never heard of doing anything like that. But for some reason I thought about those two numbers, 17.7 and 717. So, I got out my Bible and thought, *Well, I'm just going to see what the 177th verse in the Book of Genesis is*. As I looked up this verse, I was confused. I kept looking at the verse and thinking something was wrong. This is crazy. The 177th verse of the Bible is Genesis 7:17. That's right—7:17! I could hardly believe what I was looking at! Then, I started reading what all of this was about. Here are the verses: "Now the flood was on the earth forty days. The waters increased and lifted up the ark, and it rose high above the earth," (Genesis 7:17 NKJV). Obviously, this story is about Noah and the ark. So, I kept reading. In the next chapter, just a few verses later, the Bible has this to say: "Then the ark rested in the seventh month, the seventeenth day of the month, on the mountains of Ararat," (Genesis 8:4 NKJV).

Back to the prophecy spoken over me when I was in my forties. The Word of the Lord spoken was, "The status quo will longer do for you; I'm going to take you to a place, and when you get there, you will know that it was My hand that put you there and not another." Now back to Genesis and Noah's ark. The waters covered the earth, cleansing it of all evil. The waters lifted up the ark and moved it from where it was to another place. It rested upon Mount Ararat on the seventh month and the seventeenth day of the month. Do you know what the name "Ararat" means? It means "reverse the curse." God was using this trial to take me from where I was to where He wanted me to be! And in so doing, He was reversing the curse of this sickness off of me!

The last maintenance chemo treatment was scheduled for June 13, 2022. As things were winding down, I sensed for some time that the Lord was going to do something special on 7/7/2022. I was not gong to try to make anything happen, I just sensed the Lord saying to me, "Just wait and see." As I said, the last treatment was scheduled for June 13, 2022. Then I had a dermatologist appointment that led to a small procedure—totally changing the schedule. As I was rescheduling my very last chemo treatment, Dr. W's office assistant emailed me and said, "He can see you July 6-8th. I have a 10:15 on the seventh if you'd like it?" Yes, 7/7/22. I'm not making this up. I responded with, "The seventh will be just fine."

I went in for the final chemo treatment exactly two years to the day after being diagnosed and exactly 2.5 years from the very first endoscopy I had on January 7, 2020. And to top it all off (this is the most amazing date yet), it was on the exact date I rededicated my life to the Lord 49 years earlier on July 7, 1973!

On August 2nd I went in for a follow-up PET Scan. A couple of days later, I met with Dr. W. and his assistant. Dr. W. said the scan looked fine. It was everything we had hoped for. My emotions got the best of me and I couldn't hold back the tears. He said that, unlike me, many people do not choose to learn about cancer and therefore blindly leave everything up to the doctors and treatment. I told Dr. W. that we had tried to position ourselves for the best results. I told him that I had always believed there was my part and God's part; He wouldn't do my part, and I couldn't do His. I think he agreed with my approach! On the way home as Pam drove, I read the scan report. There was nothing to report...not even a single SUV (the values that show cancer activity) number listed! This was the best report I had ever received! What a great God we serve! I had to share the news and the following email was soon released:

Hey Gang,

Just wanted to report more victory to The Victory Team! After the final chemo treatment July 7th, I had a follow up PetScan this past Tuesday. I went in to get the results today from Dr. W. & it was the BEST SCAN REPORT YET!!!! Very clean!!! Everything we had hoped for Dr. W. said! ALL PRAISE to the WORTHY NAME of Jesus; our Savior & HEALER!!!!!!!

Who is like the LORD? He IS Strong & Mighty! Faithful & TRUE! KING of Kings & LORD of Lords!

A few years ago I was studying where blind Bartimaus was on the roadside while Jesus was walking by. As He cried out to Jesus those around told him to be quiet, (you know the story). However, the Bible says he cried out "all the more." The Greek word for "all the more" meant he screamed like a wild animal! You know what happened when he cried out like that? Jesus stood still; He stopped & told them to bring Bartimaeus to where He was & healed him!

As our church approaches 21 days of prayer, call on Him...be desperate for Him, cry out to Him & watch Him answer our sincere, fervent prayers for the lost, for children, for families, for healing & supernatural miracles! Let's live EVERYDAY to make it count for the Lord!

Thank you for ALL your prayers & support...Pam & I love you all!

I am now starting my 50th year of being a Christian. It is my year of jubilee! And what a year it has started out to be! As the chemo treatments are now behind me, I feel like I am standing at this threshold of a new beginning. The Lord has brought me back from death to life. Not long ago, as I was reading my Bible, I felt impressed by the Lord to do something different during my devotion and prayer time. It was like the Lord was saying to me, "When you read your Bible, jot down just a few points that stand out to you. Then, pray those points that you wrote down." While studying that week, I did just that. In so doing, I started seeing something about the numbers six and seven. Six is the number of man and describes man's efforts. Seven is divine perfection and manifestation. I thought about how I had tried to position myself for the best opportunity for healing by doing my part. Again, there are things in the natural realm that we have the means and power to do. Then God does the supernatural, the things we can't do. I thought about how the number eight comes next. *Hmm, I wonder what the number eight means,* I thought. Well, guess what? The number eight in the Hebrew alphabet is the letter "Chet." It means new beginnings. The letter is actually in the shape of a door!

Yes, I believe the Lord is leading me through a doorway, a new chapter in our lives that will reveal even more of His greatness as we encounter His new adventures and experience His exploits. I love Him more than ever before and have never felt more alive and grateful for ALL He has done and is doing! You see, with the Almighty help of the Lord, I am not going to draw back in the midst of life's storms because He will use them to make us better!

ABOUT THE AUTHOR

After just completing his 46th year, Rick continues to work as a Manufacturing Engineer for a large food can company in North America. He is married to his wife Pam, and they have two married children, Stone and Carman. Rick and Pam attend Church of the Highlands in Fultondale, Alabama.

Made in the USA
Columbia, SC
16 May 2023

16798397R00070